DO IT YOURSELF WITH ALUMINUM

DO IT YOURSELF
WITH ALUMINUM

125 PROJECTS
FOR THE HOME CRAFTSMAN

BY G. W. BIRDSALL

McGRAW-HILL BOOK COMPANY, INC., New York, Toronto, London

To my wife, Ruth

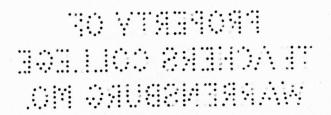

PREFACE

This book presents a wealth of shop kinks and short cuts to help the home craftsman get the most out of that fascinating new material, "Do-It-Yourself Aluminum." Here are recommended methods for fabricating this metal with the ordinary woodworking tools found in any home workshop.

The section on fastening shows how to join aluminum sheet, rod, bar, and tube in various combinations and to other materials. The chapter on surface finishing presents many types of mechanical finishes especially suitable for use with aluminum. Instructions for painting, enameling, varnishing, and lacquering are also included.

The many work projects in this book are designed to cover the widest possible variety of interests. You will find things for almost every room in the house, projects to enhance the convenience and beauty of your home. Refer to the Table of Contents on the following pages, and the Itemized Cross Index, page 131.

The author deeply appreciates the cooperation of Palma-Knapp, industrial designers, Chicago, who supplied many of the exclusive designs, and the many people at Reynolds Metals Company who made this book possible, including D. P. Reynolds, Keen Johnson, D. F. Beard, C. L. Manning, John Fox, R. J. Saurs, S. W. Miller, and Howard Wills.

G. W. BIRDSALL

CONTENTS

SECTION THREE: COST ESTIMATING AND SPECIAL
SOURCES OF MATERIAL

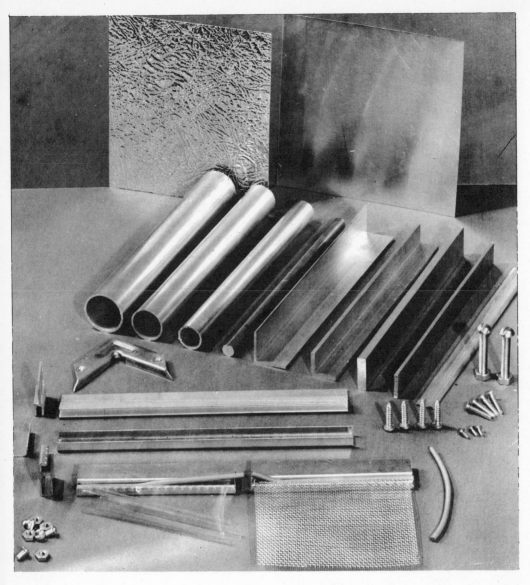

Chapter 1 . . .

"DO-IT-YOURSELF ALUMINUM"

....THE MATERIAL

LIKE other metals, aluminum has many advantages over wood in that it does not warp, rot, mildew, split, splinter, or crack. No knots detract from its perfectly uniform cross section. It already has a beautiful, naturally attractive surface that is smooth and satiny. So many projects require no surface finishing at all.

Aluminum, however, is not a single metal but a whole family of metals. There are many different aluminum alloys, each available in several different tem-

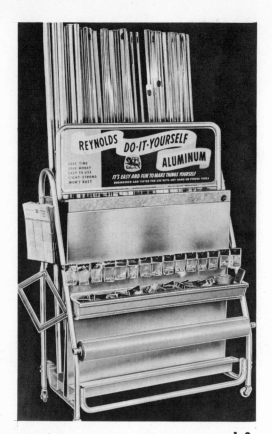

1-2

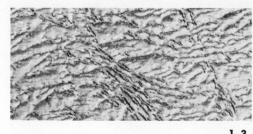

1-3

1-4

1-5

pers. Thus aluminum is made in hardnesses ranging from material nearly as soft as lead to material much harder and stronger than structural steel.

The manufacturer * of "Do-It-Yourself Aluminum" selected and engineered a particular alloy and temper so that ordinary woodworking tools can handle this aluminum without any damage to the tools. It is especially suitable for use in home workshops. Leading manufacturers † of hand and power tools have tested and approved it.

Figure 1–1 shows the basic forms of Do-It-Yourself Aluminum. More than 11,000 hardware stores, lumberyards, and building-supply outlets all over the country display it in special racks (*Fig. 1–2*).

* Reynolds Metals Co., Louisville 1, Kentucky.

† Delta, Disston, Black & Decker, Stanley, De Walt, Skil Corp., and others.

Every piece of this aluminum carries a Do-It-Yourself Aluminum identification sticker. See Chap. 15 for cost data. The various forms of Do-It-Yourself Aluminum available include the following items:

SHEET comes with a plain smooth surface, or embossed or perforated in several different designs. All sheet measures 36″ x 36″ and is a single thickness (0.020″) except for certain perforated patterns which are 0.025″ as noted below.

EMBOSSED SHEET is made in three different patterns . . . . leather grain (*Fig. 1–3*), wood grain (*Fig. 1–4*), and the square pattern (*Fig. 1–5*).

PERFORATED SHEET is available in four patterns . . . . cloverleaf perforations in stucco-embossed aluminum 0.025″ thick with 49 per cent of its area open (*Fig. 1–6*), round-hole perforations in plain

1–6

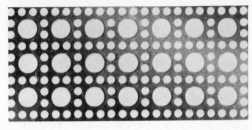

1–8

1–7

1–9

sheet with 12 per cent open area (*Fig. 1–7*), lincane perforations in plain sheet with 43 per cent free air space (*Fig. 1–8*), and union jack perforations in plain sheet 0.025″ thick with 40 per cent open area (*Fig. 1–9*).

BAR STOCK is in two sizes . . . . ⅛″ x ¾″ and ¼″ x 1″. Six-foot lengths are standard, but eight-foot lengths are also available on order if your dealer does not stock them.

ANGLE: Two sizes . . . . ¾″ x ¾″ x ⅛″ and 1″ x 1″ x 1/16″ . . . . 6′ and 8′ lengths as above.

TUBE: Three sizes . . . . ¾″ outside diameter by 0.049″ wall thickness, 1″ O.D. x 0.049″, and 1¼″ O.D. x 0.058″ . . . . 6′ and 8′ lengths as above. Spring-actuated snap-in end plugs and locking-type flanges (*Fig. 1–10*) and other fittings are available for each size tube.

ROD is a single size, ⅜″ diameter. It is available in both 6′ and 8′ lengths.

In addition to the above standard shapes, several special sections are carried to facilitate construction of window screens and storm sash.

WINDOW SCREEN SECTIONS include a special framing section for use with the plastic spline, another frame section for use with the aluminum spline, and various brace or cross members, along with drive-in clips and locks for connecting both types of frame members at the corners, as well as hangers, hooks, and eyes for mounting screens. All sections are made in both 6′ and 8′ lengths.

CLEAR PLASTIC FILM used with the above screen sections to make storm windows comes in roll form 36″ wide and 0.004″ thick.

STORM SASH: The extruded section for making glass storm windows comes in 5′,

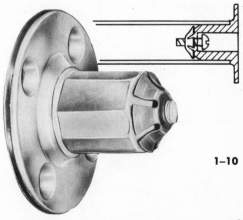

1–10

3

6′, and 8′ lengths to assure minimum loss in fitting to windows. Corner braces, hangers, and accessory hardware are in kit form.

TRIM STRIP, 5/8″ x 0.025″ x 6′, is a decorative strip used for edging tables and wall panels.

FASTENERS: To join these aluminum members, the Do-It-Yourself racks (*Fig. 1–2*) carry a wide assortment of aluminum fasteners, including round-head machine screws and bolts in five sizes . . . . 8–32 x 1/4″, 10–24 x 1/2″ and 3/4″, 1/4″–20 in 1″ and 1 1/2″ lengths; panhead sheetmetal self-tapping screws . . . . #6 in

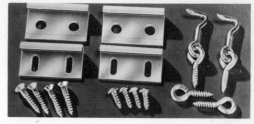

1–11

3/8″ and 1/2″, #8 in 3/4″ and 1″; brazier-head rivets . . . . 3/32″ x 1/4″, 1/8″ x 3/8″, and 1/8″ x 3/4″.

ACCESSORY KITS group various accessory items, such as for mounting screens (*Fig. 1–11*), or the corner braces, screws, and associated items required to build and mount storm sash.

Chapter 2 . . .

SHOP KINKS AND SHORT CUTS

. . . . recommended methods for fabricating Do-It-Yourself Aluminum with ordinary woodworking tools in the home workshop.

MARKING: Be sure the surface is free from oil and dirt. Use an ordinary pencil of medium softness (2B or 4B). For embossed sheet, a softer pencil (6B) or a crayon will be better, as this rougher surface is more difficult to mark. A sharp nail or metal scriber will also work well on all smooth surfaces, but avoid a deeply cut mark as it will weaken the material. Also, it will be difficult to remove when finishing the surface.

To transfer a pattern or design directly to an aluminum surface, use ordinary carbon paper and a fairly hard pencil (4H or 6H). For irregular outlines, simply fasten the pattern to the sheet aluminum with rubber cement and then cut through both pattern and sheet at the same time.

CUTTING: Use ordinary shears (*Fig. 2–1*) to cut plain, embossed, or perforated aluminum sheet. Do not use scissors that have the pivot point close to the finger grips; instead select "kitchen" or "household" shears having the pivot halfway or more toward the blade tips. This type provides more leverage and makes cutting easier.

Avoid closing the shears completely when cutting, as this will cause the sheet to wrinkle where the tips of the blade twist the metal. Where many long cuts are involved, tin snips with angled blades permit working above the sheet surface, as in *Fig. 2–2*.

When cutting an outside corner, make the first cut past the exact corner (or into it from an outside edge) as in *Fig. 2–3*. Then remove the shears from the cut and make a second cut from the outside directly toward the other side, forming the corner as diagrammed in *Fig. 2–3*. This

2-1

2-2

2-4

CUT THESE EDGES
WITH CHISEL

CUT THESE EDGES
WITH SHEARS

2-5

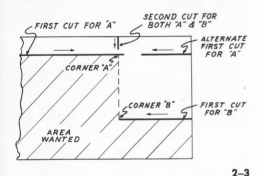

FIRST CUT FOR "A"

SECOND CUT FOR
BOTH "A" & "B"

ALTERNATE
FIRST CUT
FOR "A"

CORNER "A"

CORNER "B"

FIRST CUT
FOR "B"

AREA
WANTED

2-3

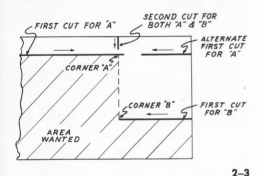

2-6

avoids distorting the sheet which would occur if you just turned the shears at the corner and continued the first cut. For the same reason, use two cuts as shown when making an inside corner.

A Boy Scout knife or ordinary pocket knife will cut burrs from tube, bar, rod, or angle stock as in *Fig. 2–4*. It will also cut sheet without damaging the blade. Simply score heavily several times, and then break the sheet apart on the cut line. The knife will cut slight arcs as well as straight lines.

Various sized wood chisels are also useful in cutting sheet. *Figure 2–5* shows a typical cutting pattern for a continuous hinge. For cuts extending in from an out-

side edge, shears are handiest. But for making internal cuts . . . . cuts that do not extend to the sheet edge . . . . the chisel works best.

Back up the sheet aluminum with scrap wood. Use a hardwood scrap, as the harder the wood, the less the chisel will distort the edge in cutting.

HAND SAWING: Any wood handsaw cuts aluminum satisfactorily, providing the saw has at least 11 teeth to the inch. Coarser saws cut roughly and tend to hang up on the metal edges when sawing tubing and the like, so they are not recommended.

Keyhole saws (*Fig. 2–6*) and ordinary wood handsaws will work, but feed lightly and use a fast stroke. When cutting tubing with a regular wood handsaw, use

5

2-7

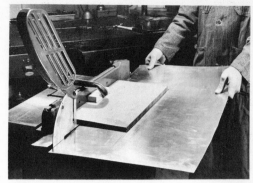

2-10

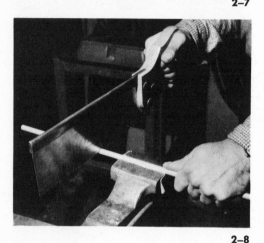

2-8

2-11

2-12

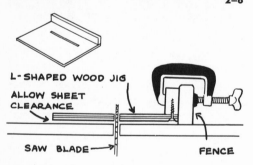

L-SHAPED WOOD JIG

ALLOW SHEET
CLEARANCE

SAW BLADE

FENCE

2-9

short, fast strokes and only the half of the blade nearest the handle to avoid "bucking." Slacken up on cutting pressure as the cut nears the halfway mark because the saw teeth may tend to lock over the tube walls.

For this reason, many craftsmen prefer to cut tubing with a saw having finer teeth, such as the ordinary hacksaw.

The coping saw (*Fig. 2–7*) is especially recommended for cutting the miters in the screen and storm-window sections and other light work such as sawing out openings in sheet.

The backsaw (*Fig. 2–8*) is especially suitable for cutting aluminum because of its rigid blade and fine teeth. It is used exclusively by manufacturer's representatives demonstrating Do-It-Yourself Aluminum.

To eliminate any tendency toward chattering or dragging when sawing aluminum, lubricate the blade with a paraffin block or an old candle stub.

POWER SAWING: For making straight cuts in aluminum sheet, an ordinary circular saw (bench saw) is hard to beat. To prevent chatter and to hold the sheet onto the worktable, make an L-shaped wood jig as shown in *Fig. 2–9*. Lower the saw blade below the level of worktable, and clamp this jig to the rip fence with a C-clamp as illustrated in *Fig. 2–10*. Start the saw, and raise the blade till it extends up into or through the jig as in *Fig. 2–9*. The jig should clear the surface of the worktable just enough to allow the aluminum sheet to slide through easily as the cut is made.

2–13

This jig also provides increased safety. It holds the sheet to the worktable and helps to confine chips. For your own safety, always wear glasses or a safety shield over your face when using any power tool. Be sure to obtain and mount on your equipment every possible safety device such as the guard on the saw in *Fig. 2–10*.

For the same reason, sweep your shop floor frequently to remove any shavings or scraps that might cause you to slip or lose your balance. A rubber floor mat in front of every power saw and power drill is well worth its slight cost because of the sure footing is helps provide.

To cut off lengths of tubing, rod, bar, or special shapes on a bench saw, clamp a 1″ x 4″ wood board to the miter gauge of the saw so that it supports the work on both sides of the cut as in *Fig. 2–11*. This helps prevent jamming by keeping the entire length of material in line till the saw cut has been completed. When working with tubing, be sure to grip it tightly to prevent the saw from rotating it when starting the cut.

Any type of circular saw blade is well suited to cutting aluminum. However, always remember to advance the metal into the saw slowly and evenly. While it is entirely practical to make long, heavy cuts in aluminum, as when ripping bar or angle sections, it is important to avoid continuous cutting with a heavy feed. This heats up the saw-blade tips and

causes them to pick up aluminum particles which partially weld to the blade.

To prevent such metal pickup, stop the feed intermittently and allow the blade to run unloaded for a short time to keep it cool. Also, while the blade is at rest, lubricate it and the teeth with a paraffin block or old candle to reduce friction. Check the set of your saw if it tends to bind after lubricating.

If the saw drags when making a heavy cut, stop it and inspect the blade. Remove any aluminum particles sticking to the teeth by flipping off with a knife or screwdriver. A wire brush is also excellent for cleaning saw teeth. Then reduce your rate of feed to avoid "leading up" the teeth again.

When jig-sawing aluminum sheet, a thin piece of wood under the aluminum helps obtain a smooth cutting action. Where a number of pieces of sheet are to be cut to the same outline, stack cutting on a band saw is preferred. Nail five or six sheets of aluminum of the required size to a scrap piece of ¼″ plywood. Mark out the cut desired on the top sheet, and get your outline by sawing down through the entire stack.

For such work, always lubricate the saw blade thoroughly with paraffin or wax from a candle before sawing. This will stop chatter and eliminate much friction and drag.

PLANING EDGES: After cutting sheet with shears or a saw, use a small wood block plane or the larger type (*Fig. 2–12*) to trim the edge or to get a straight, square-cut edge. Do-It-Yourself Aluminum will not damage the plane. A light cut will produce best results.

An ordinary wood jointer-planer (*Fig. 2–13*) does the same job much faster. For hand planing, clamp the sheet between two pieces of wood to support the edge as in *Fig. 2–12*. When using the jointer, a scrap block of wood is helpful in holding the sheet edge squarely into the cutter blades.

After ripping angles or bar stock with a saw, it is always desirable to smooth the rough saw cut. A standard jointer-planer handles this work well with no danger to the cutters, as Do-It-Yourself Aluminum will not damage the sensitive blades. Do not take more than a fine cut. To remove more metal, repeat the cut. Use a push bar to advance the work slowly and uniformly without getting your fingers too close to the cutters.

DRILLING: Use ordinary wood bits for Do-It-Yourself Aluminum. When working with a portable electric drill, center-punch the exact location desired to prevent the drill point from "traveling" before it bites into the metal. The drill must be held perfectly perpendicular to the surface, or it will tend to drift sidewise when drilling comparatively heavy sections such as bar, rod, angle, or tubing.

Chatter enlarges the hole diameter, causes drifting, and produces an irregular hole. Avoid chatter by lubricating the drill point with thin oil . . . . 10W or 20W auto oil thinned slightly with kerosene.

2–14

Lubrication is especially important in deep drilling on a drill press. Flood freely when attempting small deep holes as when drilling the holes edgewise through the 1″ bar to make the tool rack (*Fig. 6–5.*)

To drill such holes without lubrication, mount the work in a vise so that the metal particles tend to fall out of the hole as shown in *Fig. 2–14*. Back the drill out frequently to clear the hole.

Do all drilling in aluminum at high speed, the maximum obtainable on your

2–15

equipment. However, apply light feeds to avoid excessive burrs, chatter, and drifting.

An ordinary push drill will make holes in aluminum but is not recommended. Instead, use a rotary-type hand drill, a portable electric drill, or a drill press.

Excessive feeds, failure to lubricate properly, or simply failure of cut metal particles to clear out of the hole will cause the drill point to pick up metal which will partially weld to it. To prevent this, use light feeds, back out the drill frequently to clear the hole, and lubricate freely so flutes will clear metal particles from the hole.

Welding is evidenced by failure of the drill to advance under continued uniform pressure. If this happens, remove the drill from the hole. Shut it off. Clean off any metal particles from tip and in the flutes. A wire brush will usually work fine. If welded tightly, loosen with knife blade or screwdriver.

In all drilling, clamp work securely to prevent drill from twisting it. This is an important safety precaution, regardless of type of drill used. *Figure 2–15* shows a convenient way to clamp angle sections for drilling, using a piece of scrap wood under the angle.

High-speed steel drills cut cleaner and stay sharper longer than carbon-steel drills. Power wood bits of the type shown in *Fig. 2–16* drill 1/8″ x 3/4″ and 1/4″ x 1″ bar easily, providing a pilot hole is first drilled for the tip.

An ordinary brace and bit cuts holes cleanly in sheet aluminum when backed

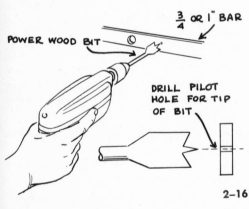

2–16

up with a scrap of wood. First punch a hole clear through the metal for locating and starting the lead screw on the tip of the bit. Hold bit steady and perpendicular to the metal surface so the bit will cut the sheet cleanly on first contact. The bit will remove a circular section of metal (*Fig. 2–17*).

Cut larger holes in the same manner, using an expansion bit, a circle cutter, or gasket cutter of size desired.

Minimize burrs on edges of drilled holes by using light feed pressures in all drilling. When using a portable power or hand drill, wobbling the drill slightly after penetrating the metal will often re-

move burrs. Otherwise, use a hand countersink for removing burrs. Or take a larger size drill and use it as a countersink under finger pressure alone.

COUNTERSINKING aluminum rod, bar, or angle permits "invisible" riveting with finished rivet heads flush with metal sur-

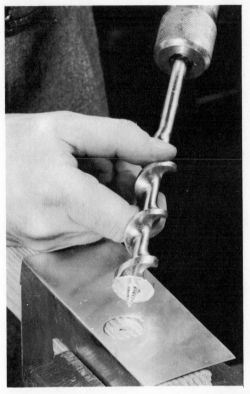

2–17

face (*Fig. 4–1*). Use an ordinary wood countersink bit in an electric drill, brace, or a drill press. Lubricate for best results. For utmost precision, clamp work in vise under drill press and use depth stop.

PUNCHING holes instead of drilling is highly recommended when joining sheet-metal parts with self-tapping screws. Place the sheet over a block of soft wood with the end grain up. Punch with a sharp nail . . . . or use an ice pick.

The value of a punched hole over a drilled hole is that it provides more metal to engage the threads of the screw. This makes possible a much stronger connection.

3–1

3–2

Chapter 3 . . .

BENDING, FORMING, SHAPING

TURNING SHEET EDGES: For making flanges (a 90° bend) or folds (180° bend), slot a block of wood and hold it in a vise while bending the sheet with the edge in the saw slot (*Fig. 3–1*) or use the forming block in your hands with the sheet against the top of the workbench as in *Fig. 3–2.*

HEMMING SHEET: Notice that one edge of the forming block (*Fig. 3–3*) is cut back at an angle to allow bending the sheet past 90° (*Fig. 3–4*). This facilitates making folds, which then are completed easily by closing the bend with a hammer, using the block to prevent denting, as in *Fig. 3–5.* Folding over the edge of a sheet in this manner is often called "hemming," and the folded-down portion is known as a "hem."

The block is slotted to the desired depth on a bench saw. If this tool is not available, make a similar block by nailing two thinner ones together using washers to space them apart to provide the slot desired.

BENDING SHEET: To make bends in center area of a large sheet, use C-clamps to hold two forming blocks against the metal (one on each side of sheet) at the point of bend (*Fig. 3–6*). Hold boards in hands, and force sheet against bench top to make bend. Hammer down on boards to sharpen the bend.

Long pieces of sheet should be clamped between boards of sufficient length to secure sheet tightly along entire length of bend. For sharp bend, hammer the edge

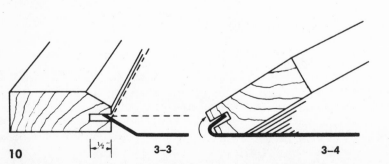

10

|← ½" →|

3–3

3–4

3–5

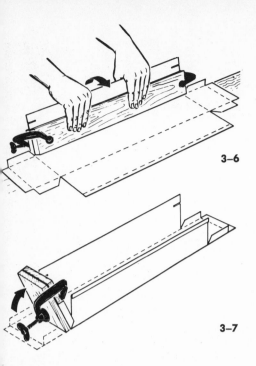

3–6

3–7

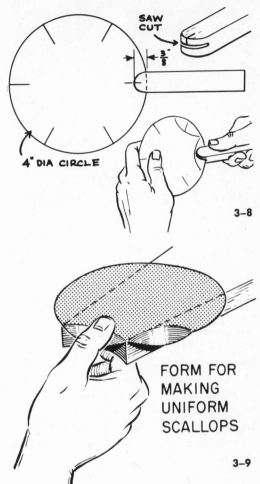

SAW CUT

4" DIA CIRCLE

3–8

FORM FOR MAKING UNIFORM SCALLOPS

3–9

while clamped over a sharp hardwood bending block.

To make a bend of unusual contour or to bend entirely around a board such as a window sill, clamp the metal over a form block and hammer with a rubber mallet or plastic-faced hammer to get the shape wanted.

Box Sections: When making a box from a single piece of sheet, the ends and sides are bent up, with flanges for locking the corners. To avoid interference when making the various bends, bend up the sides first, as in *Fig. 3–6.* Then cut scrap block just the length of the end. Clamp this to end section of box and bend up ends, as in *Fig. 3–7.* Remember to always bend up flanges and bend down folds before attempting to bend up sides and ends.

To prevent tearing of the metal at the intersection of the sides, ends, and bottom of the box section, drill a $\frac{1}{32}''$ or $\frac{1}{16}''$ diameter hole through the sheet at this intersection point.

Scallops: To create fluted edges or scallops around the edge of trays, coasters, and the like, bend up the edge at regular intervals with a slotted scrap of wood as in *Fig. 3–8,* or use the fingers to bend the

edges down over a radiused block as in *Fig. 3–9.*

For a 4″ diameter coaster, the fluting tool in *Fig. 3–8* should have a notch $\frac{3}{8}''$ deep, and the block in *Fig. 3–9* a 2″ radius and a 2″ portion of the circumference to obtain six uniform scallops. For other sizes of circles, make the block radius and portion of the circumference used equal to the radius of the circle.

Curling Sheet: Cut a slot entirely through a dowel rod or broom handle with a scroll saw as in *Fig. 3–10* or cut slot halfway through rod with a circular saw. If the latter method is used, attach a C-clamp on the end of rod to get a secure grip on it while feeding to saw blade.

Insert the sheet edge to be curled into the slot, clamp in a vise, and bend as in

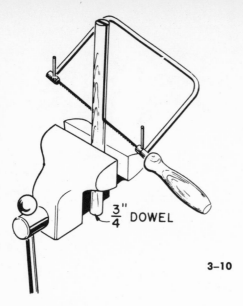

3-10

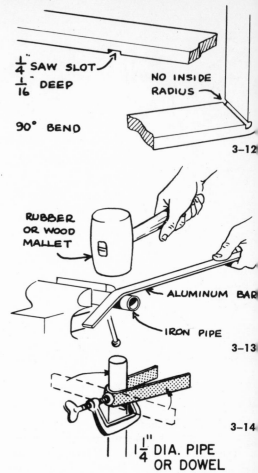

$\frac{1}{4}$" SAW SLOT
$\frac{1}{16}$" DEEP

90° BEND

NO INSIDE RADIUS

3-12

RUBBER OR WOOD MALLET

ALUMINUM BAR

IRON PIPE

3-13

3-14

1$\frac{1}{4}$" DIA. PIPE OR DOWEL

$\frac{3}{4}$" DOWEL

Fig. 3–11. Or use a C-clamp to tighten sheet in the slot, and hold the sheet against the top of workbench while rotating slotted rod with your hands.

BENDING BAR: Either $\frac{1}{8}$" or $\frac{1}{4}$" thick bar will bend easily if clamped securely in a mechanic's vise and hammered with a heavy rubber mallet while applying bending force with free hand. Cover vise jaws with scrap aluminum sheet to avoid marring bar.

For a sharp 90° bend on the inside of $\frac{1}{4}$" bar where strength is not too important, notch the bar on a bench saw as shown in *Fig. 3–12* before bending.

FORMING BAR: To make small-diameter circles, hammer bar around a sturdy round object such as a large water pipe held in a vise (*Fig. 3–13*). The $\frac{1}{8}$" x $\frac{3}{4}$" bar is curved around tubing easily if firmly anchored to it first by a C-clamp as in *Fig. 3–14.*

3-11

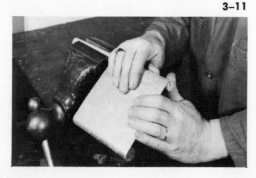

A slot cut in the end of an iron pipe makes a good bending jig for rod or bar. Hold the pipe in a vise, and bend the rod or bar around the pipe by hand (see *Fig. 3–15*). To make a sharp bend, hammer in the vise. For a soft curve, bend around a pipe as in *Fig. 3–16.*

MULTIPLE BENDS: A dowel-rod jig (*Fig. 3–17*) is excellent for bending and forming the $\frac{1}{8}$" x $\frac{3}{4}$" bar where exact dimensions are desired with two or more bends involved. Such a jig is valuable where a number of pieces are to be formed exactly alike. The successive bends are made in the jig one at a time by inserting the dowels in sequence as the bending progresses.

FORMING SCROLLS: Cut plywood circles of size desired. Drill out a hole big enough to accommodate one end of a C-clamp.

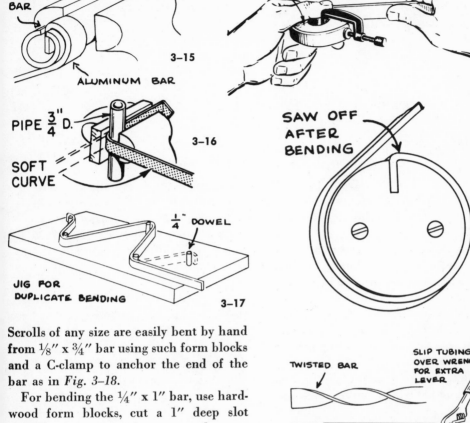

SLOT IN IRON BAR

ALUMINUM BAR

3–15

PIPE 3/4" D.

SOFT CURVE

3–16

JIG FOR DUPLICATE BENDING

1/4" DOWEL

3–17

PLYWOOD

3–18

SAW OFF AFTER BENDING

3–19

Scrolls of any size are easily bent by hand from $\frac{1}{8}$″ x $\frac{3}{4}$″ bar using such form blocks and a C-clamp to anchor the end of the bar as in *Fig. 3–18*.

For bending the $\frac{1}{4}$″ x 1″ bar, use hardwood form blocks, cut a 1″ deep slot radially into circumference, and screw securely to bench top. Insert end of bar in this slot, and bend as in *Fig. 3–19*.

SPIRALED BAR: Both $\frac{1}{8}$″ x $\frac{3}{4}$″ and $\frac{1}{4}$″ x 1″ aluminum bar make attractive ornamental spirals. Simply clamp one end in a bench vise, and twist the other end with a large wrench. To prevent "snaking" and to keep spirals straight and even, slip 1″ outside diameter tube over $\frac{3}{4}$″ bar or $1\frac{1}{4}$″ tube over 1″ bar before twisting, as in *Fig. 3–20*.

Twist sufficiently to obtain a uniform spiral, but do not overtwist. Remember, one full twist (360°) produces two spiral edges as shown in *Fig. 3–20*. To make parts with matching spirals, count twists exactly . . . . as two full twists, $2\frac{1}{2}$ or 3 or $3\frac{1}{2}$, etc. . . . . for each matching part.

SHARPENING OR FLATTENING ANGLES: Both the $\frac{1}{8}$″ x $\frac{3}{4}$″ x $\frac{3}{4}$″ and the $\frac{1}{16}$″ x 1″ x 1″

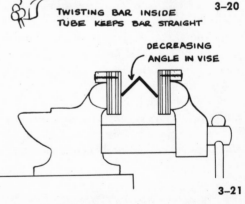

TWISTED BAR

SLIP TUBING OVER WRENCH FOR EXTRA LEVER

TWISTING BAR INSIDE TUBE KEEPS BAR STRAIGHT

3–20

DECREASING ANGLE IN VISE

3–21

angles sometimes require adjusting the 90° to some other value for certain projects, such as the exhaust hood in *Fig. 7–2*.

Figure 3–21 shows how to close the 90° angle; *Fig. 3–22*, how to open it. This method will provide accurate work if you count the exact number of turns on the vise handle. If the legs of the angle section become distorted, drive them through

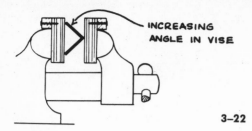

INCREASING
ANGLE IN VISE

3-22

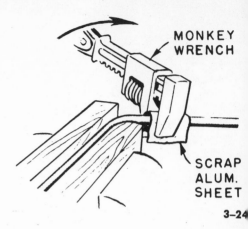

MONKEY
WRENCH

SCRAP
ALUM.
SHEET

3-24

a saw slot cut lengthwise in a scrap piece of 2″ x 4″ about 12″ to 16″ long.

BENDING ⅜″ ROD: Face the jaws of a mechanic's vise with small pieces of ¼″ plywood, hardwood preferred. This will prevent marring the ⅜″ rod when clamping for bending by hand as shown in *Fig. 3-23*.

Pull up tightly against the wood while making the bend with the hands. Rod will assume a natural radius of bend. To duplicate this natural radius when making several pieces or when bending two curves to match, place hands the same distance from the vise and apply bending force in same amount and direction. For sharp bends, hammer with a rubber or wood mallet while applying bending force with the hand.

FORMING ⅜″ ROD: To make other than a plain 90° bend, as for the legs of the nesting table (*Fig. 11-13*) use a wood plane or a wood rasp to produce the exact curve desired on a form block. Then wrap the rod around this block while clamped in a vise as in *Fig. 3-24*, using a monkey wrench as shown for precision forming.

For compound forming where more than one curve is wanted, clamp two large

wood screws or ¼″ diameter bolts in a vise. Make the first bend as shown in *Fig. 3-23* or *3-24*. Then make the second bend or curve as shown in *Fig. 3-25*, the first bend accurately positioning the second bend.

PRECISE ROD BENDING: Various projects involve a number of lengths of ⅜″ rod with 90° bends on each end, all to exactly the same dimensions. To make such rods match perfectly, drill a hardwood block to the depth required for the bend. Saw a slot part way through this block as in *Fig. 3-26*. Cut all rods to exact over-all length. Insert rod end into jig full depth, and clamp in vise. Slot allows vise grip to be applied to rod. Make the bend freehand, or hammer down with a rubber mallet if a sharp 90° bend is desired.

Where the end of the bent rod will be longer than the distance easily handled in a block, drill the hole clear through the block. Then mark rod where bend is to start, and insert rod through hole in jig until bend mark comes even with top of

3-23

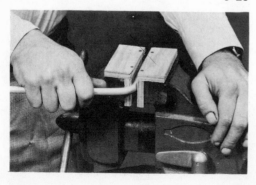

3-25

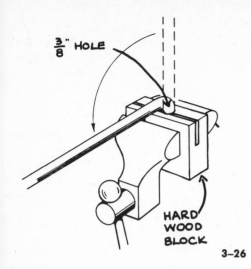

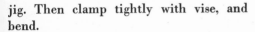

3–26

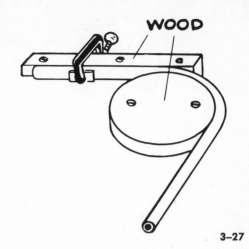

3–27

jig. Then clamp tightly with vise, and bend.

SHAPING ROD TIPS: Pointed, round, or smooth flat tips are easy to shape on an ordinary disk sander. Ends of bar, tube, and angle stock can be shaped in same manner.

GRINDING ROD, BAR, TUBE: As a general rule, avoid prolonged grinding of aluminum on a regular emery wheel because the "gummy" characteristic of the metal tends to load up the wheel, especially with heavy feeds. A power sander, either disk or belt type, is much superior for shaping aluminum. With a fairly coarse abrasive, loading will be no problem, yet cutting will be clean and fast.

TUBE BENDING: *Figure 3–27* shows the simple jig which makes tube bending easy . . . . a straight "back" block and a form block. Anchor both securely to bench top, and space just far enough apart to accommodate the size tube to be bent. There are two things to do to prevent the tube from "kinking" when bending is attempted . . . . first, clamp it securely to the back block, preferably using two or more C-clamps. Use a scrap block of wood between clamps and tube; otherwise clamps will simply collapse the tube when they are tightened. For best results, saw a V lengthwise in the face of both back block and clamping block to reduce the

tendency of clamping pressure to collapse the tube.

Second, use a clamp block long enough to wedge up against the form block. This will prevent any tendency of the clamp block to slide and allow the tube to move. *Warning*: Any movement of the tube lengthwise as you apply the bend will result in kinking and a spoiled piece of material.

To prevent tube collapse at the bend, avoid using too small a bend radius. Recommended minimum radius for ¾″ tube is 2½″ when packed with sand, 5″ if unpacked; for 1″ tube, about 4¾″ packed, 9½″ unpacked; for 1¼″ tube, 5½″ packed, 11″ unpacked. These are safe minimum radii even for the inexperienced, providing the accompanying instructions are followed.

Packing the tube with sand helps prevent collapse and so permits radii about half those practicable without packing. Poke the tube up and down in a bucket of semiwet sand. If sand does not tamp well into tube, it probably is too wet; add more dry sand to mixture. If it tamps in but falls out, it may be too dry. Tap tube on concrete floor or sidewalk to pack sand down firmly. After bending, shake out sand or wash out with a hose.

For best results, the surface of the form block around which the tube is bent should be turned on a lathe or worked with a wood rasp to the same radius as the contour of the tube (⅜″, ½″, or ⅝″, respectively, for ¾″, 1″, and 1¼″ tube). This contacting jig surface will then support the tube better and prevent collapse. With skill and such a jig, appreciably smaller radii than those listed above become practicable.

Most important . . . . when making bends without sand, screw jig to bench top so tube sticks straight out over edge of bench at start of bend. Use your body and left hand to apply bending pressure as you start the bend, and with your free right hand strike sharp blows with a heavy rubber mallet on tube exactly over the point where bending is occurring. This helps the metal to upset on the inside of the bend and so keeps the bend smooth and uniform without collapsing. Watch as you make the bend . . . . if tube tends to collapse, stop further bend movement while you hammer vigorously to work the metal and control tube contour. Then renew your bending action . . . . work slowly. With a little practice you can easily make smooth, small-radius bends without difficulty.

Chapter 4 . . .

JOINTS AND FASTENING METHODS

GENERAL: This chapter presents methods for joining the various pieces of Do-It-Yourself Aluminum to each other and to other materials. It shows many types of joints and how to make them. These joint details are collected in this chapter to avoid repeating them again and again where the same joint appears in several different items.

For projects exposed to the weather continuously, such as awnings and lawn furniture, always use aluminum fasteners to avoid dissimilar metal corrosion. If it is necessary to use other metals for certain parts such as bolts, hinges, or reinforcing angles, be sure to coat them with aluminum paint or clear lacquer before assembly. Paint or enamel is also suitable.

Joints in window-screen sections and storm-window sections are detailed in free instruction sheets available at all hardware stores handling Do-It-Yourself Aluminum, so directions are not repeated here.

RIVETING is widely used because it offers a permanently tight fastening that is easy to make, inconspicuous, and reliable. To avoid movement sidewise between members joined, drill rivet holes just big enough to insert the rivet. Where several rivets are used in a single joint, drill hole for one rivet only; insert and head up that first rivet; then drill the next hole and head up that rivet; and so on. This assures correct hole alignment.

Use vise or C-clamps to hold members exactly in position desired. Then drill

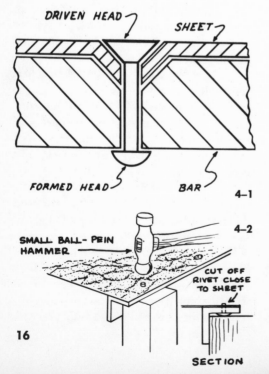

DRIVEN HEAD — SHEET —

FORMED HEAD — BAR — 4-1

SMALL BALL-PEIN HAMMER — 4-2

CUT OFF RIVET CLOSE TO SHEET

SECTION

through both members to be joined. Avoid attempting to drill matching holes before assembly. After drilling, clean off any metal upset or turned up around the edge of hole.

Every rivet comes with a head already on one end .... the "formed" head. You must make the head on the other end .... called the "driven" head. Insert the rivet, and position the work with the formed head against a heavy solid object such as a vise or metal block. Obtain a block of iron or steel for this purpose from your local scrap yard or any welding shop .... 1″ x 2″ x 4″ is a convenient size. Hold this backup block against the formed head while you upset the driven head. For easy access, put the formed head inside when working on box sections.

Obtain the correct amount of metal to make the driven head by cutting off rivet shank so that it extends *through* the work a distance $1\frac{1}{4}$ to $1\frac{1}{2}$ times the rivet diameter.

Be sure parts to be joined are clamped together tightly before upsetting the rivet.

Start to form the driven head by striking on the end of the rivet several blows directly in line with the rivet shank. This upsets the rivet shank to make it fill the rivet hole completely. Use flat face of hammer for this operation.

Now use the ball-peen face of the hammer to strike blows directly in line with the rivet shank but around the edge to form the metal down and around the work. Make the driven head look like the formed head.

INVISIBLE RIVETING of sheet to bar or angle is accomplished by countersinking the heavy member on the surface next to the sheet, which is then forced down into the depression so formed. The driven rivethead then fills this depression, giving a smooth level surface on top. See *Fig. 4–1* for details.

In another method (*Fig. 4–2*) used with leather-embossed sheet, cut the rivet shank off close to the sheet and work

edges of rivet over hole in sheet with a small ball-peen hammer. Touch up with steel wool. Done carefully, the pattern on the end of rivet will blend with the embossed sheet pattern.

REMOVING RIVETS: A misplaced or badly driven rivet is removed easily by center-drilling through the head of the rivet with same sized drill used for the original rivet hole. To locate the hole accurately, file a flat on the top of rivethead and carefully center-punch exact center to start drill properly.

SELF-TAPPING SCREWS: To join sheet to sheet with self-tapping screws, drill top sheet with hole large enough to clear screw. *Punch* hole in lower sheet, as this

ALUM. TAPPING SCREW

MORE HOLDING AREA

4–3

will provide double the holding power as compared with drilling. *Figure 4–3* indicates punching with a nail. An ice pick is also excellent. Use a wood block for backup to avoid deforming sheet.

To fasten sheet to a plaster wall, first drill all the holes in the sheet large enough to pass a #8 x ¾″ self-tapping screw .... the size recommended. Then position sheet on wall, and drill into plaster through the center of two of these guide holes, going clear through the plaster with a #32-size wire drill.

Then insert screws in these two holes, being careful to hold them steady and guide them straight into the hole. Exert a steady pressure while screwing into hole. Do not set up screw too tightly, or it will break plaster. If drilled and the screw driven properly, plaster will not break out and the screw will provide excellent holding power.

With first two screws in place, drilling and driving the remainder are easier, as the sheet is now held securely in position.

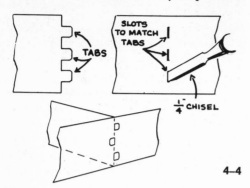

4-4

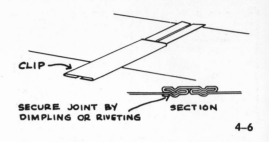

SECURE JOINT BY DIMPLING OR RIVETING

SECTION

4-6

SLOTS AND TABS (*Fig. 4–4*) are handy for joining many sheet parts. Cut slot with ¼″ chisel as shown. Use shears and chisel for cutting tabs as directed in *Fig. 2–5*. After inserting tabs, lock joint by bending them over in opposite directions, wherever possible.

SHEET EDGES: To join two sheets, turn up a flange and fold it part way down along the edge of both sheets. Interlock the two folds and hammer flat with a wood block (*Fig. 4–5*). In this joint, one sheet is at a higher level than the other at the joined edge.

To keep the sheets at the same level, turn both folds up and use a slide clip to join them as in *Fig. 4–6*. Lock either joint by dimpling or riveting or with sheet-metal screws.

CORNERS OF BOX SECTIONS: Many projects employ box sections where the bottom of the box, the two ends, and the two sides

are cut from a single piece of sheet. After flanging up the sides and ends, locking the corners completes the box section.

The most widely used corner connection (*Fig. 4–7*) employs bolts or rivets to hold a flange on one member to the adjacent member. A corner lock that uses neither rivets nor bolts is the double-bend lock shown in *Fig. 4–9*. Make this connection in two stages as shown.

A third method (*Fig. 4–8*) employs a simple corner clip locked to the members to be joined on the inside of the corner by means of folds as shown. Make this assembly first with folds only partly closed; then hammer them tight, using a wood block to prevent marring the metal. Dimple with punch.

To make the clip, cut a piece of sheet 1½″ wide and as long as height of the corner of box. Bend in middle with form block, and then bend back ⅜″ from each edge.

CONTINUOUS HINGE: Make two sets of interlocking tabs by first marking out one set on the edge of one member. Make tabs ⅜″ long, 1″ wide, 1⅛″ between tabs. Cut

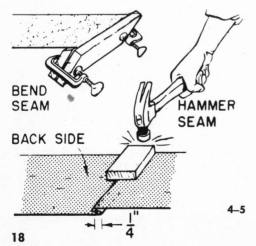

BEND SEAM

BACK SIDE

HAMMER SEAM

¼″

4-5

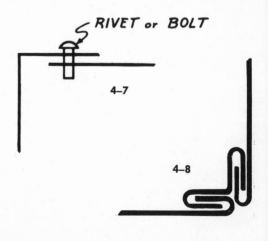

RIVET or BOLT

4-7

4-8

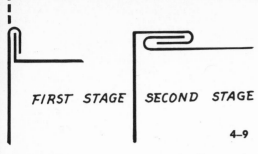

FIRST STAGE | SECOND STAGE

4-9

with shears and chisel as in *Fig. 2–5.* Use this set of tabs to mark outline of matching set of tabs on the other member. Cutting just inside this outline provides proper clearance between the two sets of tabs in the hinge.

Now flange up both sets of tabs 90°, and interlock them with a piece of wire coat hanger or aluminum clothesline wire between them as in *Fig. 4–10.* Turn down tabs over wire with screwdriver as shown. Complete the forming with pliers (*Fig. 4–11*) to make the finished hinge.

TIPS FOR ⅜″ ROD: Rubber crutch or cane tips of ⅜″ inside diameter make excellent tips for end tables and other projects using rod for legs. Obtain them at your local hardware or variety store. To modernize the shape, slip the tip over a short length of ⅜″ rod and rotate the rubber tip against a sanding disk to cut off extra rubber, leaving a smooth cone-shaped tip. Shorten the tip in the same manner where desired.

Small tack-type hard-rubber glides or bumpers also provide fine tips for use on ⅜″ aluminum rod. Drill ⅛″ diameter hole ½″ deep in end of rod. Drive in a hardwood plug. Then drive tack-type bumper or glide into the wood.

ROD CONNECTIONS

MACHINE SCREWS: *Figure 4–12* shows rod "A" T-connected to another rod "B." Drill "A" to pass 10–24 machine screw. Drill and tap "B" to take 10–24 aluminum screw. This same T-joint can also be used with sheet, bar, or angle at "A." The rod-to-tube connection (*Fig. 4–13*) is also made the same way. Note that one tube wall has a ⅜″ hole, the opposite hole

4-10

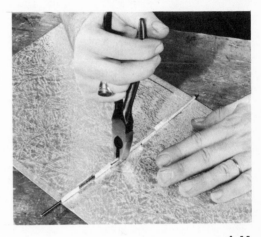

4-11

"A"

"B"

4-12

being just large enough to pass the 10–24 machine screw.

In all these connections, set up screw tightly, file off top portion of head down to bottom of screw slot, and peen edge of screwhead down over "A."

A rod-to-rod end connection (*Fig. 4–14*) uses a length of stud bolt obtained by cutting off the head of a ¼″ –20 machine

19

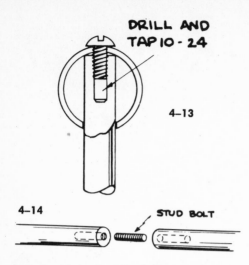

DRILL AND
TAP 10-24

4-13

4-14

STUD BOLT

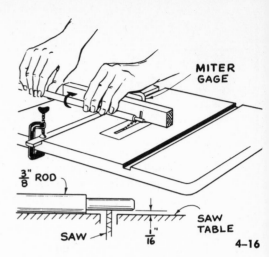

MITER GAGE

3/8" ROD

SAW

SAW TABLE

1/16"

4-16

screw, with rod ends drilled and tapped to fit.

BOLTED SWIVEL (*Fig. 4–15*) provides a movable joint where motion of the two members is involved. Peen end of bolt over nut to lock it in place. A rivet may be substituted for the bolt if desired.

REDUCING ROD END: Where a rod end is to be threaded for a connection or fitted through a hole for upsetting to make a rivet-type end connection as shown below, it is necessary to reduce the end of the rod to a smaller diameter. An easy, quick method is illustrated in *Fig. 4–16*. Use a C-clamp to hold the miter gauge of bench saw so that the rod is positioned directly over saw blade which is adjusted to provide a $\frac{1}{16}''$ cut. Rotate rod over blade, and move lengthwise to obtain length of cut desired. The $\frac{1}{16}''$ cut will reduce rod to $\frac{1}{4}''$ diameter for making $\frac{1}{4}''$ x 20 threads. Use a $\frac{3}{32}''$ cut to reduce the rod to $\frac{3}{16}''$ diameter for riveted joints.

THREADED CONNECTIONS: When rod end is reduced as detailed above and threaded with $\frac{1}{4}''$ x 20 threads, the rod can be screwed directly into $\frac{1}{4}''$ x 1" bar which has been drilled and tapped to fit (*Fig. 4–17*). Let end extend through slightly, and peen over to lock joint. Sections of $\frac{1}{4}''$ bar can be made into ornamental nuts easily.

For $\frac{1}{8}''$ x $\frac{3}{4}''$ bar and for sheet and angle, use a nut and washer to make the T-connection as shown in *Fig. 4–18*. This same connection can be used with tube by drilling one wall $\frac{3}{8}''$ diameter and bolting through opposite wall similar to *Fig. 4–18*. The riveted connection (*Fig.

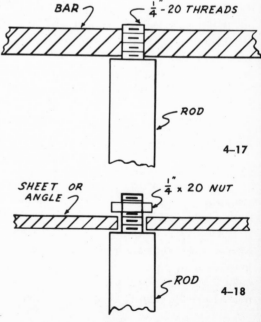

BAR

1/4"-20 THREADS

ROD

4-17

SHEET OR ANGLE

1/4" x 20 NUT

ROD

4-18

SWIVEL

4-15

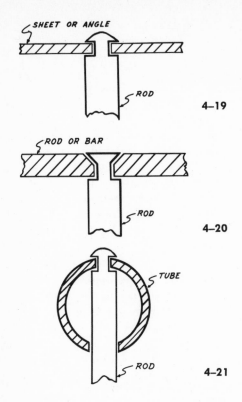

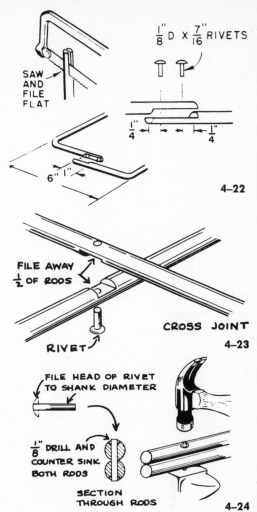

4–21) makes a stronger joint with tube and is recommended over the threaded joint.

END-RIVETED CONNECTIONS: The simplest method of connecting rod to sheet is the end-riveted T-joint (*Fig. 4–19*). Here a $\frac{1}{8}''$ length on the end of the rod has been reduced to $\frac{1}{4}''$ diameter by the method of *Fig. 4–16*, inserted through a $\frac{1}{4}''$ hole in sheet, and riveted by peening the extended portion of rod. The same joint is also suitable for connecting to $\frac{1}{8}''$ x $\frac{3}{4}''$ bar cr to $\frac{1}{16}''$ x 1'' x 1'' or $\frac{1}{8}''$ x $\frac{3}{4}''$ x $\frac{3}{4}''$ angle.

The connection can be made "invisible" when end-riveting rod to rod or to $\frac{1}{4}''$ x 1'' bar by countersinking top member of the T-joint and upsetting end of rod into this area (*Fig. 4–20*), filing off excess metal, and polishing with steel wool.

To end-rivet rod to tube, drill $\frac{3}{8}''$ hole in near side of tube and $\frac{3}{16}''$ hole in far side. Then reduce about $\frac{3}{16}''$ length on end of rod to $\frac{3}{16}''$ diameter (per *Fig. 4–16*), insert it, and upset extended portion as indicated in *Fig. 4–21*.

RIVETED JOINTS: *Figure 4–22* shows how to join rods end to end by halving and overlapping. Countersink holes in rod, and work rivetheads over to make flush with surface. To accommodate rod curvature, nip off excess material in formed rivethead before driving rivet.

For securing rods that cross each other, notch and rivet as shown in *Fig. 4–23*. The side-by-side joint (*Fig. 4–24*) uses a $\frac{3}{4}''$ x $\frac{1}{8}''$ rivet with head cut off lengthwise to retain full length. Insert in $\frac{1}{8}''$ holes, and hammer opposite ends alternately to upset both evenly. File away excess metal, and polish area with emery cloth or steel wool to produce an invisible joint.

Follow these same instructions to make invisible joints to connect rod to bar and bar to bar.

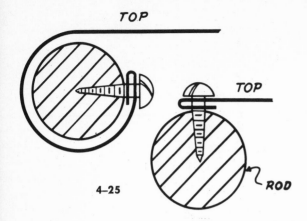

TOP

4-25

ROD

TOP

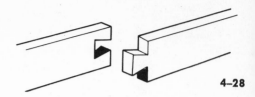

4-28

SHEET TO ROD: Use self-tapping sheet-metal screws to attach sheet to rod. Always hem edge of sheet (per *Fig. 3–5*) before attaching. Screws can be on underneath sheet surface, or on top of sheet and rod, as in *Fig. 4–25*.

BAR CONNECTIONS

END-TO-END BAR JOINTS . . . . LAP TYPE: Lap joints are suitable for joining $\frac{1}{4}''$ x $1''$ bar stock. In *Fig. 4–26*, the bar is halved in thickness. In *Fig. 4–27*, the bar is halved widthwise on opposite ends. In both, when assembled and countersunk riveted, the joint will be practically invisible. A $\frac{3}{4}''$ to $1''$ overlap is recommended. After cutting and fitting joint (*Fig. 4–27*), clamp the two members to-

gether in position and drill two holes edgewise to fit two finishing nails which are used as rivets. Cut heads off the nails, and cut them about $1\frac{1}{16}''$ long. Drive into place, and upset both ends. File off excess metal, and hammer flush. Done carefully, the complete joint will be practically invisible.

END-TO-END JOINTS IN BAR: The simplest design is a plain butt joint with a splice plate riveted or bolted to the back side. To make the rivets invisible, countersink the bar on the outside surface and drive rivets flush. To assure matching holes, use a C-clamp to hold one bar and splice plate in position while drilling the first hole. Then rivet. Next drill second hole in these two parts, and rivet.

Now clamp splice plate to second bar, drill first hole, and rivet. Then remove clamp, drill and rivet second hole. Use the same procedure if bolting the connections.

For a dovetail joint (*Fig. 4–28*), use coping or hack saw or jigsaw to cut one element. File to finish the joint surfaces accurately. Then use a sharp nail or scriber to mark out matching element

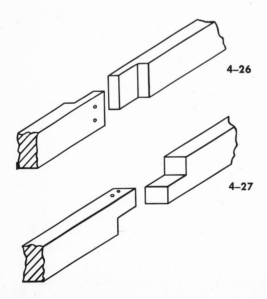

4-26

4-27

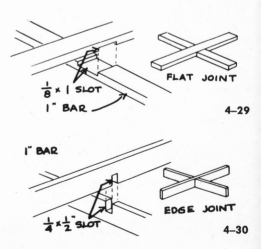

$\frac{1}{8}$ x 1 SLOT

1" BAR

FLAT JOINT

4-29

1" BAR

$\frac{1}{4}$ x $\frac{1}{2}$" SLOT

EDGE JOINT

4-30

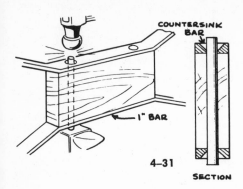

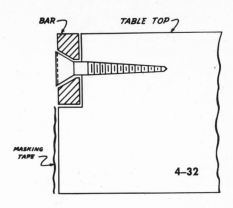

from this first part. Cut matching element slightly oversize, and file to exact fit.

After making the dovetail joint and assembling it, lock it by drilling a small hole edgewise through the joint and driving in a small pin (nail). If joint edges do not match perfectly, close them by peening lightly. Follow with file, sandpaper, and steel wool to make adjoining surfaces match.

X-JOINTS IN BAR: For a neat lapped joint in $\frac{1}{4}''$ x $1''$ bar, use either the flat joint (*Fig. 4–29*) or the edge joint (*Fig. 4–30*). Notch each bar to prevent endwise movement of either piece. For most accurate work, saw the slots slightly undersize and then file to exact fit. These same joints work with $\frac{1}{8}''$ x $\frac{3}{4}''$ bar also.

BOLTING BAR TO BAR: To make aluminum boltheads "invisible" when joining two bars face to face, countersink the upper surface to a depth equal to about one-third the thickness of bolthead. After bolt is pulled up tightly, peen the head into the countersunk opening, file off excess metal, and polish with fine emery cloth.

On many occasions, just filing off top of heads down even with the bottom of the screwdriver slot will greatly improve the finished appearance of the joint.

Many times the excess bolt length will break off easily with a pair of pliers, avoiding tedious sawing. Whenever cutting bolts to shorter lengths, thread nut onto bolt first and saw to length. Backing off nut then recuts any damaged threads and partially removes burrs.

BAR-SPACER-BAR: To attach $1''$ bars to both sides of a wood spacer block (as in the coffee table of *Fig. 11–6*), alternately peen the $\frac{3}{8}''$ rod into recesses countersunk in both bars as shown in *Fig. 4–31*. Make joint invisible by filing off excess metal and polishing with fine emery cloth.

EDGING WITH BAR: Often it is desirable to inset the edge of a table with an aluminum bar. *Figure 4–32* shows how to do this with flathead aluminum wood screws in such a manner as to permit the fastening to become invisible ($\frac{1}{4}''$ x $1''$ bar).

The trick is to countersink the outer surface of the bar just the right amount, enough so that when the screw is pulled up tightly in the hole, the bottom of the screwdriver slot in the screwhead will lie just above the surface of the bar.

Then file off the extruding portion of the head perfectly smooth and even with the bar. To avoid any minute cracks around the periphery of the screw, use a small ball peen hammer to work the metal in the edge of the screw out to fill the countersunk portion of the bar completely . . . . after filing has progressed almost even with the bar surface. Then finish filing.

When insetting bar in an outer rail, as in making the table of *Fig. 8–1*, use masking tape to cover the adjacent portions of the rail while filing to prevent marring these surfaces.

Finish the filing with a fine file, and then rub with fine emery cloth or steel wool to give the screwhead and bar surfaces a matching appearance.

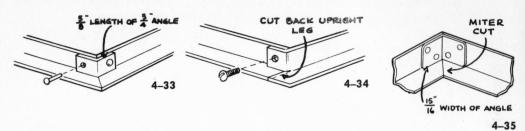

4-33

4-34

MITER CUT

$\frac{15}{16}$" WIDTH OF ANGLE

4-35

ANGLE CONNECTIONS

CORNER JOINTS IN ANGLES: *Figures 4–33* and *4–34* show easily made corner joints in $\frac{1}{8}$" x $\frac{3}{4}$" x $\frac{3}{4}$" angle. Either bevel ends or overlap ends. Saw off a $\frac{5}{8}$" length of $\frac{3}{4}$" angle for the corner splice in *Fig. 4–33*. Bend around and overlap vertical leg in *Fig. 4–34* to secure joint. Bolt or rivet either joint. Both these designs are suitable for use where the vertical leg is on either the outside or the inside of the corner.

For $\frac{1}{16}$" x 1" x 1" angle, cut a splice plate from the same stock and rivet either inside (*Fig. 4–35*) or outside the vertical legs. Use two $\frac{1}{4}$" x $\frac{3}{32}$" rivets on each leg to prevent twisting.

The design of *Fig. 4–36* avoids twisting by using a long overlap as shown. For added strength on both joint designs, rivet a flat, triangular gusset plate to the horizontal legs inside the corner as in *Fig. 4–37*.

CORNER BENDS IN ANGLES: Notching, then bending, is best way to get angle stock around a corner. That method is usually preferred to making a joint at a corner because there is no interruption of metal in the outer surface. The following instructions are for working $\frac{1}{16}$" x 1" x 1" angle: To provide enough metal to make the bend without cracking, always drill a $\frac{3}{32}$" hole exactly at the corner, as shown in *Fig. 4–37*. This hole must be right up against the outer leg of the angle. Then for 90° corners make two 45° cuts into the drilled hole as shown. File sawed edges smooth and straight where best appearance is desired.

Place the unnotched leg of the angle in a mechanic's vise with the point of bend exactly at edge of vise jaws. Now pull the

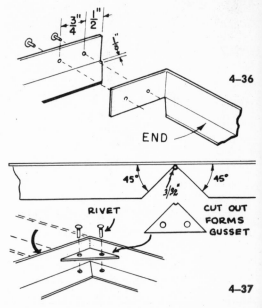

END

4-36

RIVET

45° 45°

$\frac{3}{32}$"

CUT OUT FORMS GUSSET

4-37

angle around the bend with your hand, lightly tapping the metal at the bend with a wood or rubber mallet as you complete the bend. For an entirely closed notch, use a small steel hammer to work metal shut as you complete the bend.

This method provides a sharp, clean corner bend with a completely closed notch in the $\frac{1}{16}$" x 1" x 1" angle as shown in *Fig. 4–38*. The added thickness in $\frac{1}{8}$" x $\frac{3}{4}$" x $\frac{3}{4}$" angle necessitates a different method as follows:

Determine the exact position of corner. Then drill two $\frac{1}{8}$" diameter holes side by side through the leg to be notched as shown in *Fig. 4–39*. Saw through center line of holes to make two 45° cuts. Use rattail file to remove small point remaining between holes. Clamp in mechanic's vise, and bend, hammering the metal lightly to close the notch as you complete the bend. The two holes blend into one as shown in *Fig. 4–40*. If, after adjusting lengths as described below, the hole ap-

4–38

4–40

MAKE CUTS TO
CENTER OF HOLES

45°

4–39

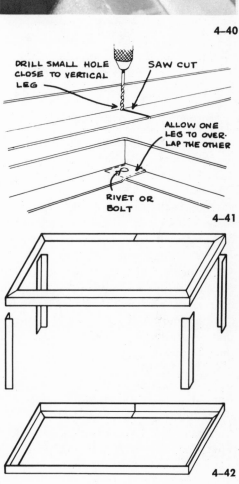

DRILL SMALL HOLE
CLOSE TO VERTICAL
LEG

SAW CUT

ALLOW ONE
LEG TO OVER-
LAP THE OTHER

RIVET OR
BOLT

4–41

4–42

pears egg-shaped or uneven, redrill it to improve its appearance.

Another type of corner bend (*Fig. 4–41*) can be made in the $\frac{1}{16}''$ x 1" x 1" angle by drilling a $\frac{3}{32}''$ hole at the bend point, making a saw cut directly into this hole, then bending the angle, allowing the horizontal members to overlap as shown. Rivet or bolt the overlapping members.

ADJUSTING LENGTHS BETWEEN BENDS: When fitting angles to table tops for trim and for other precise work, it often is desirable to change the distance between two bends slightly. This is easy with the following technique:

Secure the unnotched leg of the section that is too long in a mechanic's vise with a corner about $\frac{1}{16}''$ from the edge of the vise jaws. Clamp tightly. Then with a lightweight hammer, strike the metal directly on the corner. Being clamped tightly in the vise, the metal can move only toward the open member. As metal flows around this corner under repeated blows, the notch members will slide slightly to accommodate it.

The section of angle can be shortened as much as $\frac{1}{32}''$ or more by this method. It also works on the $\frac{1}{8}''$ x $\frac{3}{4}''$ x $\frac{3}{4}''$ angle. Redrill the clearance hole if it is distorted.

BOX FRAMING: The easiest way to construct a box frame is to bend an angle to make a complete loop for the top frame, bend another piece of angle for the bottom frame, and then join the two with vertical posts at the four corners, as shown in *Fig. 4–42*. Join abutting ends of frames with splice plates. Rivet corner post to top and bottom frames as in

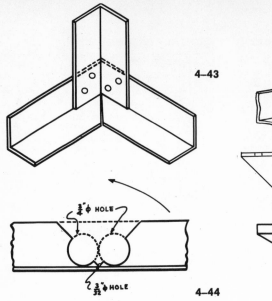

4-43

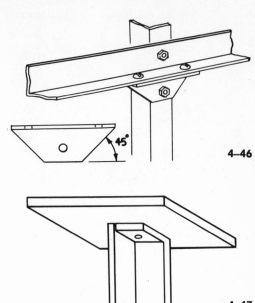

4-46

4-44

¾" φ HOLE

³⁄₃₂" φ HOLE

4-47

close-up diagram (*Fig. 4–43*). This shows the corner post inside the frames, usually the best way, although it can also be placed outside the frame if desired.

FITTING ANGLE AROUND TUBE: For certain projects like the stretchers around the lower ends of table legs (*Fig. 11–9*) one side of 1″ angle stock is cut to fit around ¾″ diameter tube. The best method of accomplishing this is to make the plain bend as detailed in *Fig. 4–37*. Then after bending and closing the notch, clamp in that position under a drill press and drill the ¾″ diameter hole exactly in the corner. Or if a drill press is not available, scribe a circle of that size in the corner and cut it out with a scroll saw. Smooth the hole edges with a rattail file.

Figure 4–44 shows another method. First drill the ³⁄₃₂″ hole exactly at the

corner. Mark 45° lines to this hole, and drill two ¾″ holes as shown. Cut out on solid lines, and bend. The two ¾″ holes will fit together to form one. *Figure 4–45* shows the completed joint . . . . ¹⁄₁₆″ x 1″ x 1″ angle around ¾″ tube. Use self-tapping sheet-metal screws to lock angle to tube.

ANGLE-TO-ANGLE JOINT: The best way to connect one angle to another in either a T-joint or an X-joint is to bolt or rivet the two adjacent legs as in *Fig. 4–46*. To brace and stiffen the joint, cut a small piece of the same type angle section and rivet or bolt it to the other members as shown.

4-45

ATTACHING ANGLE LEGS: It is easy to attach the end of an angle to the bottom surface of a table top by cutting off a section of one face of the angle and bending the other down alongside it as in *Fig. 4–47*. Then drill a hole through this, and drive a screw through it into the underside of the table top. While such a connection itself will not keep the leg from tilting, table designs using this leg connection have ample strength designed into the accompanying framework structure.

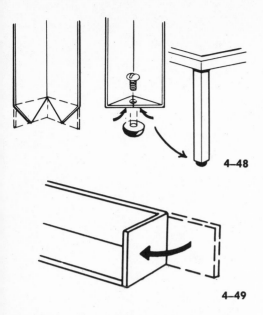

4-48

4-49

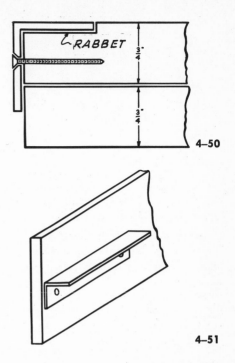

4-50

4-51

CLOSING ANGLE BENDS: When angles are used as legs on tables and various items, it is desirable to close the open ends in some way to increase the area contacting the floor and thus reduce any tendency to dig into floors or rugs. *Figure 4–48* shows how to attach a rubber bumper by cutting a pair of 45° miters on both legs of the angle and bending inward. Then drill to pass the screw attaching the bumper.

The method of *Fig. 4–49* is still easier. Simply cut off one face of the angle as shown, and bend the opposite piece of leg to overlap it.

INLAYING 1″ ANGLE: Any table top can be enhanced greatly by inlaying the edge with 1″ angle as shown in *Fig. 4–50*. Before starting to inlay, be sure table edge is absolutely straight lengthwise and square with the table top. The best way is to run edge through a jointer-planer. Then rabbet out a section ¹⁄₁₆″ deep and 1⁵⁄₁₆″ in from the corner to make the angle come flush with the table top.

Most tables will require two lengths of angle. Make the joints in the angle come in the center of table ends. Thus one piece goes along the front edge of table and half the length of each end. The second piece then goes along the back edge of table and remainder of distance at each end. It is easier to line up joints along a straight edge than at corners. Measure length required, and cut angle stock ⅛″ longer for good measure. Drill, notch, and bend corners per *Fig. 4–37*. Adjust length between bends for precise fit if necessary. Secure angle to table edge with finishing nails.

To make nailheads invisible, file off top of nailheads to cut head thickness in half. Drill a hole in angle the exact size of nail body. Then countersink slightly with a drill same size as nailhead. But remember that the table trim stock is only ¹⁄₁₆″ thick, so countersink must be very shallow, just a little less than the depth of the filed nailhead. Now position trim accurately, insert nail, and drive into table top. Use a small hammer, and drive nailhead flush with surface of the angle trim. Try one or two with scrap pieces of angle to get the hang of it.

DRAWER SLIDES FROM ANGLES: *Figure 4–51* shows an easy way to make slides for drawers inside cupboards or storage units, using ⅛″ x ¾″ x ¾″ angle with one of the flat faces up. Where a drawer is to work between table legs of angle stock,

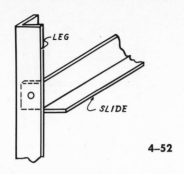

4–52

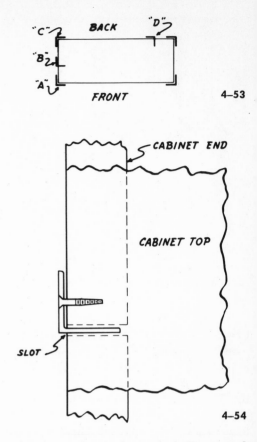

4–53

4–54

Fig. 4–52 shows how to mount the drawer slides to the legs to avoid interference. The vertical leg of the angle stock forming the drawer slide is cut ¾″ longer than the horizontal leg and then bent around back of the table leg, to which it is then riveted.

RECESSING ANGLE: In the vanity table shown in *Fig. 9–7* and in many other plywood structures such as bookcases and desks, it often is desirable to sink one face of angle stock used for framing. Most designs using angle framework look best with the flat faces of the angle legs outward . . . . thus in *Fig. 4–53*, angles used at corners for legs face front and left at "A"; back and left at "C."

But suppose you wish to set the angle in from the corner . . . . as at "B." Note from *Fig. 4–54* that the end piece of the cabinet is slotted to take the front face of the angle. Using this type of construction, back legs can also be moved in from the corner as at "D," *Fig. 4–53*.

Recessing the angle in this manner adds novelty and a modern touch and makes the item actually stronger because the panels help hold the angle rigid.

TUBE CONNECTIONS

MOUNTING LEGS made of aluminum tube is involved in such projects as the dining-room table of *Fig. 8–1* and the sawhorse of *Fig. 6–1*. The only unusual operation is *angle drilling*. Most tables use leg angles of 7° to 10° from the vertical. The sawhorse requires a 30° angle.

Do not attempt to drill these holes with a brace and bit. Always use a drill press.

Most have flat beds, and drill vertical holes only. To drill at an angle, a fixture is needed. Make angle blocks for such a fixture as follows:

Take a scrap piece of 1″ x 2″ wood, and screw through it into the end of a 10″ to 12″ length of 2 x 4. Fasten this to the miter gauge of a bench saw with a C-clamp as shown in *Fig. 4–55*. Set the miter gauge to the angle desired. Advancing the assembly to the blade will make the cut wanted as shown. Cut two blocks in this manner, and screw them along the sides of a 12″ x 12″ piece of ½″ plywood. *Figure 4–56* shows a 30° fixture of this type clamped to the bed of a drill press ready for use. Make the 7° and 10° fixtures the same way.

Mark on the surface of the work the exact center of the hole desired. Then spot the work in position accurately under the drill, and clamp it to the fixture with C-clamps as in *Fig. 4–57* (a 10° fixture).

Measure depth of hole desired, and set depth stop on drill press. Clamp work

securely to avoid wobble and enlargement of hole.

Use drills of the type shown in *Fig. 4-56*, of same diameter as tube for leg. After drilling, lubricate the tube with paraffin block or old candle before inserting. Rub lubricant lengthwise of the tube at $\frac{1}{8}''$ to $\frac{1}{4}''$ intervals around the circumference. Clamp the drilled wood securely in a vise. Insert tube with a screwing motion while pushing it into

4-56

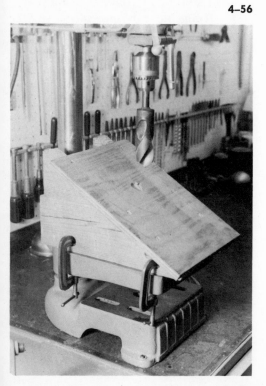

hole. Always turn tube in same direction . . . . clockwise is usually most convenient. Before inserting mark hole depth on tube so you can tell when tube has bottomed in hole.

Lock tube in place by drilling through edge of plywood squarely into tube and through it from one side or down at an angle. Then drive in a finishing nail long enough to go through tube and into wood on other side. Use a drill of the same diameter as the nail.

To obtain sufficient hole strength, depth of hole should be $1\frac{1}{2}$ to 2 times the diameter of tube. Add plywood blocks where necessary. Following are recommended minimum hole depths and thickness of plywood blocks suitable for attaching legs to underside of a table top (if you drill part way into table top, reduce block thickness accordingly): For $\frac{3}{4}''$ diameter tube, use $1\frac{1}{4}''$ deep hole (one $\frac{1}{2}''$ plus one $\frac{3}{4}''$ thickness of plywood); for $1''$ tube, $1\frac{3}{4}''$ hole (two $\frac{1}{2}''$ plus one $\frac{3}{4}''$ plywood); for $1\frac{1}{4}''$ tube, $2\frac{1}{4}''$ hole (three $\frac{3}{4}''$ plywood). Nail plywood together with finishing nails to get total thickness indicated. Make blocks to a width 3 to 4 times tube thickness, a length 5 to 6 times. Drill the hole off center lengthwise so about two-thirds of the block extends in a direction opposite the leg (see *Figs. 4-58* and *4-59*).

Where two pieces of tube are used to make a single leg, as in the dining-room

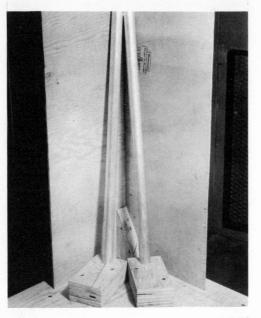

4-58

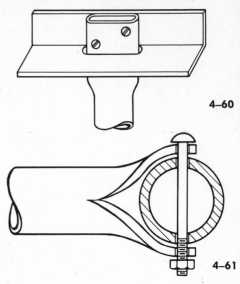

4-60

4-61

table of *Fig 8–1*, mount each tube in a separate block at a 7° angle and lock in place. Then position block on a flat surface, and cut off leg to height desired, making this cut horizontally.

To locate legs correctly under the table corner, use a jig (*Fig. 4–58*) made from two pieces of scrap plywood 12″ to 18″ wide nailed to a small block to form a 90° angle as shown. Be sure bottom edges of plywood are square to the vertical joint.

Turn table top upside down, and position jig on a corner 1″ (or 2″) inside table edges. Position the two blocks so leg tips come together inside top corner of jig and so the two legs form 30° angles as

in *Fig. 4–59*. Now put screws down through predrilled holes in the blocks and into the underside of the table top. Bolt legs together at tips by drilling down through open end of one leg.

FLATTENED-TUBE CONNECTIONS: End-to-end connections, T-connections, and X-connections are simple to make by flattening the tube at the connection and riveting or bolting members. Flatten the tube in a vise . . . . do not hammer flat.

Flattening the tube provides a surface easily connected to angle, bar, or rod or for screwing to a wood member, as well as tube-to-tube connections. *Figure 4–60* shows how one leg of an angle can be slotted or cut away to make a passage for a flattened tube connection to the inside surface of the other leg.

SLOTTED TUBE CONNECTIONS: Saw a slot into tube lengthwise. Flatten out split portion to form fingers which will go on either side of a tube, bar, or rod, to which it is attached by bolt, pin, or rivet as shown in *Fig. 4–61*. Or self-tapping sheet-metal screws can be used when connecting tube to tube. Joint will swivel if only one connector is used. Two or more will make joint rigid.

Flatten the inside tube and flatten the split outside tube just enough to go on either side of the first tube for another simple type of slotted connection.

4-59

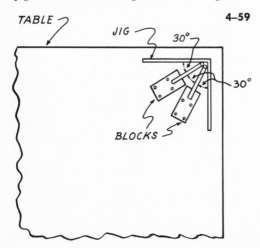

TABLE

JIG

30°

30°

BLOCKS

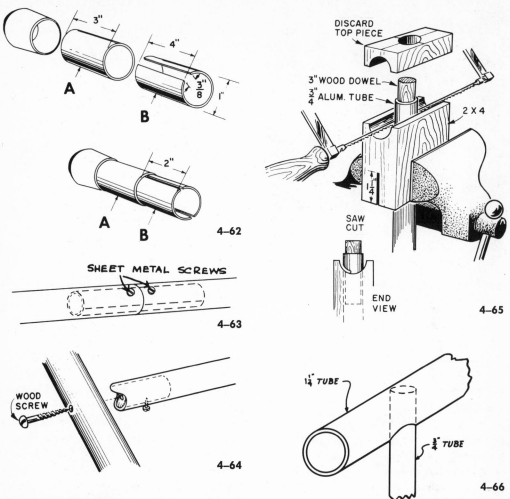

4–62

SHEET METAL SCREWS

4–63

WOOD SCREW

4–64

DISCARD TOP PIECE

3" WOOD DOWEL
¾" ALUM. TUBE

2 X 4

1¼"

SAW CUT

END VIEW

4–65

1¼" TUBE

¾" TUBE

4–66

SLIP JOINT: To connect two pieces of same size tube end to end, cut a third piece of tube 4″ to 6″ long to act as an internal "sleeve." Cut a ⅜″ wide slot the entire length of this sleeve, as at "B" (*Fig. 4–62*). Squeeze the piece so the cut edges touch, reducing outside diameter of sleeve so it will slip inside the ends of tubes to be joined. Secure sleeve to one tube with a self-tapping sheet-metal screw.

END-TO-END JOINTS: To connect two tubes of the same size permanently, join with an internal sleeve as detailed above and secure to both tubes with self-tapping sheet-metal screws (*Fig. 4–63*). Or connect with a 4″ to 6″ length of wood dowel rod. Drive part way in end of tube. Screw through tube into dowel. Then drive remainder of dowel into end of second tube and secure with screw.

T-CONNECTIONS: For joining tube to tube (*Fig. 4–64*), drive wood dowel into end of one member and screw through top T-member into it as shown. Lock dowel into first member with self-tapping screw.

To make end of dowel and tube fit contour of second member precisely, use a jig (*Fig. 4–65*). Drill holes all the way through 2 x 4's for both T-members to the size of tube being used. Cut off top of jig on center line through top hole as shown. Drive dowel into tube end, and cut exact contour with scroll saw as shown.

In another method (*Fig. 4–66*) cut hole in top member of T to take second member which is inserted in first as shown and then locked with a through bolt, a pin, or self-tapping sheet-metal screws set in at an angle close to point where second

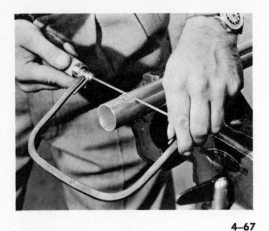

4–67

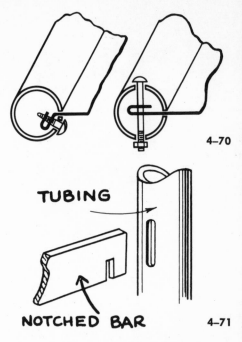

4–70

TUBING

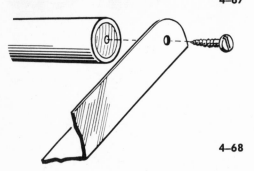

4–68

NOTCHED BAR   4–71

member enters top member. *Figure 4–67* shows how to cut hole required, using scooping action. Finish with rattail file to exact size and contour required.

For tube to bar or angle, drive wood dowel in tube end and use wood screw as shown in *Fig. 4–68.* For maximum strength, use expanding slotted dowel and bolt as in *Fig. 4–69.*

TUBE TO SHEET: Hem edge of sheet (*Fig. 3–5*), and attach to tube with self-tapping screws, either on top or wrapping the sheet around tube and screwing under-

neath as in *Fig. 4–25.* Or slot tube on bench saw. Insert hemmed edge, and secure with self-tapping screws or through bolts (*Fig. 4–70*). Or drive a wood dowel rod lengthwise through tube to lock sheet into slot. In the latter case, do not hem sheet edge.

TUBE-BAR JOINT (*Fig. 4–71*) has bar fitted into slot in tube made by drilling row of holes and smoothing with a flat file. If bar is notched as shown, joint is easily disconnected. For permanent connection, bolt clear through tube and bar.

TUBE-TO-WOOD JOINT: By notching the tube as shown in *Fig. 4–72* to make a key-

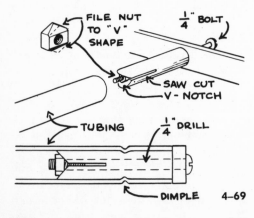

4–69

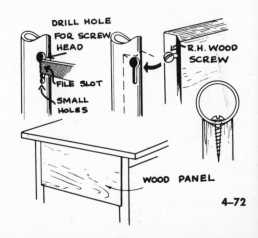

4–72

4-73

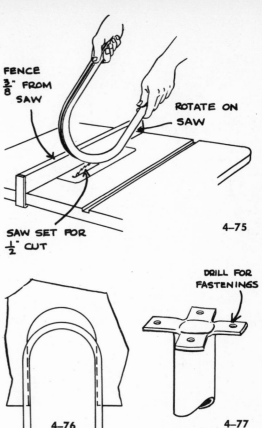

FENCE ⅜" FROM SAW

ROTATE ON SAW

SAW SET FOR ½" CUT

4-75

DRILL FOR FASTENINGS

4-76

4-77

hole-type slot, the tube is made to engage a round-head wood screw set in the bottom of the V-cut edge of a wood panel. Adjust the depth of wood screw so that tube can be driven on. Wood stretchers between table legs often employ this joint.

LEVELING SCREW, BOLTHEADS: The appearance of tube connections is greatly improved by setting down screwheads or boltheads so they do not project above the tube surface. Round off the end of a 2" length of ½" dowel rod, and use as an indenter (*Fig. 4–73*). Drill the screw or bolt hole first, and use the hole to position the indenter. Hold it directly in line with hole, and strike the indenter squarely with hammer.

For best results, support tube in a jig made by cutting a slot the same width and depth as the tube in a 2 x 4. This will prevent tube from distorting, even under repeated blows of indenter.

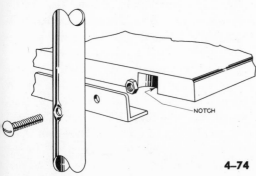

NOTCH

4-74

TUBE SHELF SUPPORT: Where a tube-and-angle frame supports wood shelving, use the design shown in *Fig. 4–74*. Bolthead is set below surface of tube by indenting (*Fig. 4–73*). Nut is hidden by a notch in end of shelf. Small flat-head wood screws up through countersunk holes in horizontal leg of the angle secure the shelf.

EDGING OPENINGS WITH TUBE: Edge the entrance to doghouse or any other opening in sheet as follows: Bend ¾" tube to contour of opening. Then rotate tube against bench saw as shown in *Fig. 4–75*. This slits the outside of tube, allowing it to slide into opening in the sheet (*Fig. 4–76*).

TUBE TO FLAT BASE: To attach a 1¼" tube to a flat object, drill four ¼" diameter holes equally spaced around the tube and down 1½" or 2" from the end. Saw slots to edge of these holes, bend down the tabs so formed, flatten them, and drill for fastening (*Fig. 4–77*).

33

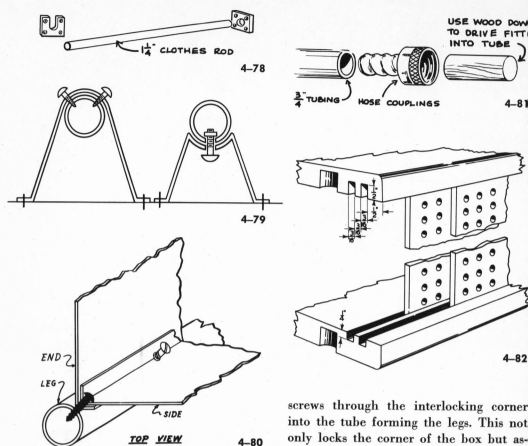

4–78

USE WOOD DOW
TO DRIVE FITT
INTO TUBE

4–8▮

3/4" TUBING   HOSE COUPLINGS

1 1/4" CLOTHES ROD

4–79

4–82

END
LEG
SIDE
TOP VIEW   4–80

TUBE TO WALL: For clothes-closet rods and similar uses, tube can be attached endwise to wall surfaces by using wood blocks (*Fig. 4–78*). The U-shaped block permits easy removal of tube by just lifting that end.

To attach a length of tube parallel to a wall for a stair rail or similar use, make a bracket to go around the tube or underneath the tube as in *Fig. 4–79*. In the latter case, attach brackets to tube before mounting to wall. Insert nuts through open tube end. Brackets are 3/4" bar.

TUBE LEGS FOR BOX SECTIONS: To put tube legs on sheet-metal box sections such as planters, flower boxes, and magazine racks, turn in a 1/4" flange on the edges of the sheet to be attached to the leg, then interlock these flanges as shown in *Fig. 4–80* and drive self-tapping sheet-metal

screws through the interlocking corner into the tube forming the legs. This not only locks the corner of the box but assures a firm connection to the leg. Install a screw every 1 1/2" or 2" along the leg.

HOSE-TO-TUBE COUPLING: *Figure 4–81* shows how to drive a standard hose connection into a piece of 3/4" tube, using a wood dowel rod to prevent damage to the coupling. This connection is handy for sprinklers, scrub-down brushes, and the like.

SLIDING DOORS can easily be inserted and removed if made from 1/8" thick tempered Masonite and set into 3/16" wide slots as shown in *Fig. 4–82*. Note that bottom slots are only 1/4" deep while top slots are 1/2" or 5/8". This allows door to be fitted into opening by inserting top of door into upper slot full depth, which then provides sufficient clearance to permit door to be placed in lower slot without falling out of opening. Here, cut door to height equal to distance between shelves plus 3/8".

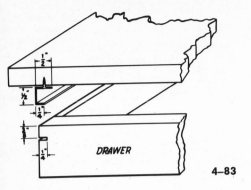

DRAWER

4-83

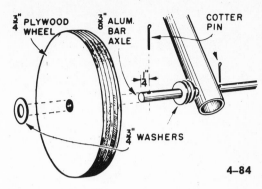

¾" PLYWOOD WHEEL ¾" ALUM. BAR AXLE COTTER PIN

¼" ¾" WASHERS

4-84

Where shelves are ¾" thick plywood and have sliding doors above and below them, reduce depth of slots to ⅛" for lower, ⅜" for upper. Door height then becomes distance between shelves plus ¼". If height of door opening is 1' or less, it may be necessary to cut upper slots slightly wider to provide sufficient clearance for easily inserting the doors in place.

SUSPENDED DRAWER SLIDES: To mount drawers underneath shelves or cabinets, form up a piece of plain aluminum sheet as shown in *Fig. 4–83* and screw to underside of shelf or other support. Then cut slots in outside faces of drawers to fit into these slides. The result is a neat, handy drawer arrangement. Drawers can be placed close together by installing drawer slides back to back.

WHEEL-AND-AXLE SET (*Fig. 4–84*) makes projects easy to move about. Axle of ⅜" rod is readily attached to tube framework of serving cart and can be made any length required. The ¾" thick plywood wheels are 4" to 6" in diameter. To seal against the weather where outdoor use is anticipated, seal the wood wheels with three or four coats of thin shellac. Then apply aluminum paint.

CEMENTING: When large areas of aluminum sheet are applied over a solid surface as on table tops, desk tops, and the like, it is best to cement the entire aluminum panel down solid to avoid projecting screwheads, rivetheads, or nailheads.

Also this prevents puncturing the sheet and thus keeps it intact to prevent leakage. Too, cementing prevents "oil canning" . . . . the same effect produced when squeezing the bottom of an oil can.

Aluminum, like all other metals, has no pores for the cement to attach into mechanically. To give the cement every possible chance to stick to the aluminum, roughen the surface with coarse emery cloth or sandpaper. This helps provide "teeth" into which the cement can "key," or anchor, itself.

Next, carefully clean off all dirt, grease, and grime by scrubbing with naphtha or dry-cleaning fluid. Likewise, see that the wood or other surface is clean. Apply cement to both surfaces, allow to partially set, and then squeeze the two surfaces together, maintaining the pressure until set. Be sure to follow detailed instructions of the maker of the cement you use.

For aluminum, a cement that remains partially "wet" is required because a hard-drying cement may break loose owing to the larger expansion and contraction characteristic of aluminum. Cements that remain tacky and so are recommended for use with aluminum include "Mastic #7 Tuff-Bond" (Goodloe E. Moore Co., Inc.) and "M-3 Cement" (Minnesota Mining & Mfg. Co.).

SOLDERING ALUMINUM is only recommended where the joint carries no mechanical load. Soldering is primarily for sealing a riveted, bolted, or mechanically interlocked joint such as *Fig. 4–5* or *4–7*.

Soldering must always be done with solder and flux especially designed for use with aluminum because this metal differs from other common metals in that it is always covered with a thin glass-like layer of aluminum oxide when exposed to air.

Ordinary soldering fluxes will not remove this oxide layer. So it is necessary to use a special flux designed for this particular work. Follow the maker's instructions to the letter. Most fluxes are designed to work with a particular solder. Be sure to use the recommended solder. Before soldering, always clean the work with sandpaper, steel wool, or a wire brush to remove all dirt, grease, and heavy oxide.

Aluminum fluxes and solders operate at temperatures up to 700°F instead of the 400–600°F range of common solders. This means the work must be heated to a higher temperature range. But aluminum conducts heat away from the soldering point rapidly so that a large heat input thus is required . . . . much higher than available from the usual electric soldering iron. Even a 250-watt electric soldering gun will heat only small thin pieces of aluminum. Use an alcohol, gas, or gasoline torch for all aluminum soldering.

These heat requirements also make it impracticable to solder large or thick aluminum parts. So avoid attempting to solder aluminum rods and bars. Do-It-Yourself Aluminum sheet can be soldered without trouble with a little practice.

In general, there are three different types of aluminum soldering methods: The "friction" method involves covering the surface of the metal at the joint with a layer of molten solder and then abrading the surface down through this layer using a sharp-pointed instrument or a wire brush to remove the oxide layer. The molten solder cover protects the aluminum surface laid bare so that the solder may bond to it. This abrading must be done carefully to assure that a sufficient portion of the area is "tinned."

In the second method . . . . "flow" soldering . . . . the flux employed chemically attacks and removes the oxide layer so that the solder can bond directly to the aluminum surface. A good flux and solder of this type will usually permit soldering with less difficulty than the first method.

In the third method, a new flux (called a "reaction" type) is employed which chemically reacts at the soldering temperature to deposit a layer of tin on the aluminum. Once covered with tin, it is easy to solder the aluminum.

Remember that the *work* must be brought up to temperature. So apply the torch flame to the work, preferably to the back or underside so that the flame does not play directly against the flux or solder. The flux will change appearance, fume, or smoke when the correct temperature is reached. Maintain work temperature while applying solder to tin the work surface.

After work surfaces are tinned, place them in position and flow additional solder in to complete the joint, being careful to apply the heat to the work, not to the solder itself.

Chapter 5 . . .

SURFACE FINISHING

NATURAL FINISH: All aluminum is covered with a film of aluminum oxide which protects the underlying metal so that aluminum needs no paint or other coating to shield it from the weather. This is why bare aluminum will not rust away as does iron and steel.

Also this naturally bright, attractive finish of aluminum is usually preferred for most projects although aluminum will take a wide variety of mechanical, chemical, and even paint finishes where desired to match other surfaces.

To preserve aluminum's natural finish, clean the surface mechanically, as detailed below, and then apply wax, producing a long-lasting finish that will not pick up finger marks or dirt.

CLEANING: Before applying any finish, free the aluminum surface of heavy accumulations of dirt, dust, grease, or grime by rubbing hard with a clean cloth. Sandpapering and rubbing with steel wool or a wire brush will also clean the surface mechanically.

To make paint, lacquer, or varnish stick to aluminum, a *chemically clean* surface is required. Even a fingerprint will prevent proper adhesion. So before painting, the mechanically cleaned surfaces must be cleaned chemically by scrubbing with naphtha, dry-cleaning fluid, mineral spirits, lacquer thinner, or any product recommended by your paint store for preparing aluminum surfaces for paint. Then paint without further handling, using care to avoid touching the clean surface with the bare fingers.

WAX: Any aluminum surface shows finger marks readily. To avoid finger marking, apply a coat of paste wax after mechanically cleaning the surface. Let dry 10 minutes, and polish with a clean dry cloth. A wax finish will protect and enhance the appearance of any mechanical finish described below.

LACQUER: Clear automotive lacquer may be used in a similar manner to retain the original high luster of polished aluminum. First spray on a mist coat. When dry, apply a heavier coating. Tinted lacquers supply exceptionally attractive effects over aluminum. Be sure the surface is chemically clean before lacquering.

PAINT: Where the aluminum may be subjected to severely corrosive conditions such as continuous outdoor exposure to salt spray along the seacoast, protecting with clear lacquer, aluminum paint, or a heavy coat of wax is recommended. If any aluminum surfaces outdoors (lawn furniture, screens, or storm windows) develop pits from corrosive attack, clean the surfaces thoroughly and apply a clear lacquer designed for outdoor service. Or paint them with an aluminum paint designed for outdoor service.

Of course, any color of paint or enamel can be used effectively with aluminum for a particular color scheme. Just be sure the aluminum surfaces are chemically clean. If possible, use a surface preparation especially recommended for aluminum before applying the paint.

MECHANICAL FINISHES are easiest to apply and produce striking effects with aluminum. Here are some of the best:

POLISHING: Use cloth buffing wheel at peripheral speed of 7,000 feet per minute with tripoli powder mixed with grease

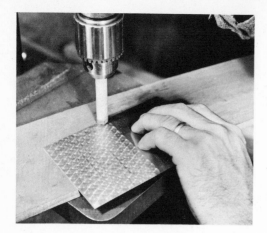

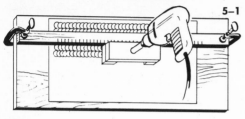

5–1

5–2

binder applied to wheel as the abrasive element. Apply light pressure. For highest gloss, follow with open muslin buff at 8,000 feet per minute, using a softer silicon abrasive compound and extremely light pressure.

For hand polishing, use automobile body rubbing compound or pumice stone and oil.

SATIN FINISH: Rub with fine steel wool, fine emery cloth, or sandpaper. Rub back and forth in one direction only. Wear plain cotton gloves to avoid finger mark-

ing while finishing. This will give a high gloss and even finish. To prevent finger marking, apply wax as above.

DAMASCENE OR WATCH-CASE FINISH (*Fig. 5–1*) is possibly the most beautiful of all the mechanical finishes. It is also known as an engine finish or sun-swirl finish. It is easy to make on plain aluminum sheet using a drill press fitted with a tool made as shown . . . . a $\frac{1}{2}''$ dowel rod with a soft rubber tip covered with fine emery cloth. Set drill press for slowest speed of tool. Touch work lightly. For the straight formal pattern shown, make contact in series of spots spaced $\frac{1}{4}''$ apart in a straight line. Then make next line overlap first by $\frac{1}{4}''$.

To do this work with a portable electric drill, the dowel tool must be fitted with a $\frac{1}{4}''$ shank by drilling the $\frac{1}{2}''$ dowel and inserting a $\frac{1}{4}''$ shank or by reducing the $\frac{1}{2}''$ dowel to $\frac{1}{4}''$ with a wood rasp or with a bench saw as in *Fig. 4–16*.

Next make the saddle block shown in *Fig. 5–2*, and drill a $\frac{33}{64}''$ diameter hole to take the dowel tool. Cut a straight edge $1'' \times 2''$ to the length desired for the setup (*Fig. 5–2*). Mark off front edge with $\frac{1}{4}''$ marks. Now ride saddle block against straight edge, and make row of spots spaced $\frac{1}{4}''$ apart along straight edge. Move straight edge $\frac{1}{4}''$, clamp, and make next row of spots.

GEOMETRIC DESIGNS: *Figures 5–3* and *5–4* illustrate two novel mechanical finishes

5–3

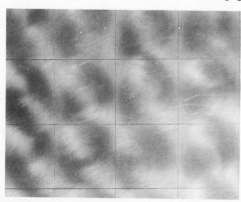

5–4

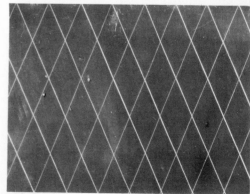

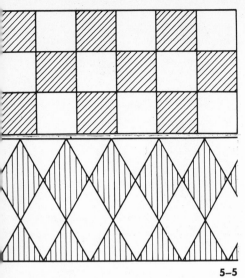

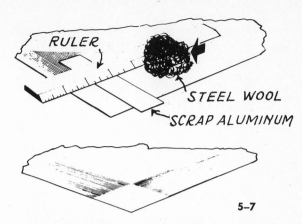

5–7

5–5

built around a geometric design. *Figure 5–3* is ruled off in 2″ squares, using a sharp nail or scriber to make a fairly deep mark. Use uniform pressure so lines themselves will be uniform. Hold scriber at right angles to straight edge, and tilt top slightly in direction of movement.

Now cut out a 2″ square in heavy cardboard to use as a mask. Place this hole over each square, one at a time, and rub with medium-coarse steel wool in a circular motion. Result is series of swirl patterns inclosed in individual squares.

Another geometric design is the diamond (*Fig. 5–4*). Space off 1″ marks along edge of sheet; then scribe a series of lines at a 60° angle up to the right and another series up to the left. They intersect to make the diamond pattern.

Squares, diamonds, and other designs may be enhanced further by *graining* alternate rows as in *Fig. 5–5*.

ROTARY SANDING: Many novel surface designs are easily produced with motor-driven sanders and rotary electric tool sets.

BALL PEENING: Hammer plain sheet with small ball peen hammer with scrap wood backing (*Fig. 5–6*). Use soft wood for deep effects, hard wood for shallow effects. Hammer with a steel plate backup to create a different effect. For a "leaf" design, use the flat portion of the hammer head.

DESIGN GRAINING: By graining (rubbing with coarse steel wool) various portions of a surface in different directions, a variety of surface designs can easily be created, using just a straightedge (ruler) as illustrated in *Fig. 5–7*.

Figure 5–8 shows how to use a simple stencil to decorate a circular item. Grain one segment, then move stencil and grain next segment, etc. This makes a safe substitute for acid etching for many projects.

5–6

5–8

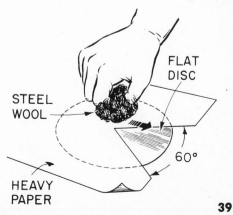

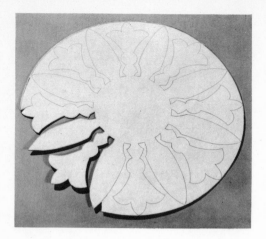

5–9

5–1

ORNAMENTAL DESIGNS

REPRODUCING A DESIGN: Make a template of heavy paper, as in *Fig. 5–9*, and use this to shield the portions of the aluminum surface which you wish to remain bright. Scrub the exposed surfaces with steel wool, sandpaper, emery cloth, crocus cloth, or other abrasive as in *Fig. 5–10*.

EMBOSSING A DESIGN: Lay out design full scale on paper, and trace through onto the aluminum, using carbon paper and sharp pencil. Then emboss it into the surface with a nail punch, as in *Fig. 5–11*, or use a screwdriver, nail, or other tool as in *Fig. 5–12*. Back up with scrap wood. Possibilities are limited only by your ingenuity.

THREE-DIMENSIONAL DESIGNS: To produce a raised, embossed, or three-dimensional design, carve a pattern into a block of hardwood 1″ or more in thickness as in *Fig. 5–13*. Place the sheet of aluminum

over the carved area, cover with an old rubber inner tube, and hammer heavily. If pattern is small, use a ball peen hammer.

The embossing can be reproduced many times without damaging the wood block. Any number of small rosettes (*Fig. 5–13*) can be made this way and cut out with scissors after forming.

ANTIQUE EFFECTS: Embossed sheet with leather grain pattern or peened or other mechanically worked sheet surfaces take a beautiful "antique" finish as follows: Select the color of paint, enamel, or lacquer desired, and apply it to the face or "front" (concave embossed) side of the sheet. When thoroughly dry, highlight by rubbing lightly with steel wool to remove paint on raised portion of the pattern, leaving it in the low spots.

This produces novel and attractive effects. It allows carrying out any desired

5–10

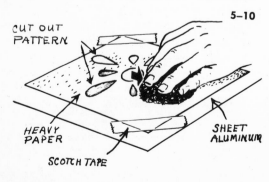

CUT OUT PATTERN

HEAVY PAPER

SCOTCH TAPE

SHEET ALUMINUM

5–12

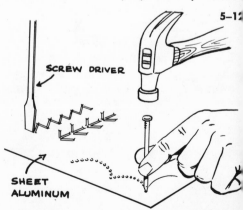

SCREW DRIVER

SHEET ALUMINUM

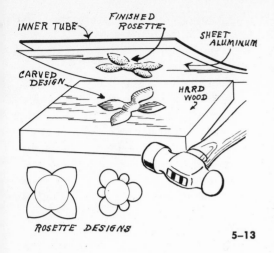

ROSETTE DESIGNS

5–13

5–14

color scheme to make the aluminum "match" its surroundings.

Another novel effect is produced by reversing the embossed sheet and applying paint to the "back" (convex or raised side) of the pattern. When coating is dry, highlight with 4/0 or 5/0 sandpaper wrapped around a block of wood. This flat sanding bares only the highly raised portions of the embossed pattern, leaving a larger area of painted metal than the first method.

FOR BAR, either ¾" or 1", strokes from the ball end of a ball peen hammer will produce an antique or wrought-iron effect when subsequently roughened with fine sandpaper or garnet paper and painted black.

To give any aluminum object a "wrought-iron" appearance, soot it thoroughly over a candle flame and hammer the soot into the surface, using steel back-up plate. Then clean off loose material with cloth or steel wool.

AVOID CORROSION: Where other metals contact aluminum for extended periods with moisture present, electrogalvanic attack may result. Thus where it is necessary to use conventional iron hardware, such as hinges or flat corner braces, apply a coat of paint, enamel, or lacquer to the hardware first before fastening it to the aluminum. Aluminum paint is ideal for this purpose.

Indoors, where everything is kept dry, pay no attention to this factor. This means that steel nails, screws, bolts, and other items can be used with aluminum parts without corrosive action resulting as long as the assembly is not wet or moist for any considerable period of time.

GROUND CONTACT over long periods may cause corrosion of aluminum surfaces, depending upon how much moisture and free alkali is in the soil. To guard against possible corrosive attack here, all aluminum in continuous contact with the earth, such as in a trellis, garden markers, and decorative borders for flower gardens, should be protected by applying one or two coats of aluminum paint to those areas to be covered with earth.

Bituminous paint also provides excellent protection. Zinc chromate, too, is a good corrosion inhibitor.

CHEMICAL ETCHING: A chemically etched surface has a soft, dull appearance which contrasts well with bright polished surfaces. So objects to be decorated by etching should be first highly polished. Sources of specially polished sheet in form of circles for trays will be found in Chap. 15.

Transfer pattern to the sheet surface with carbon paper and pencil. Cover areas to remain bright and shiny by painting with "T" asphaltum paint, black stove polish, or bituminous paint. Use two coats if necessary. A fine-tipped brush will help to reproduce design details accurately. Then fill in large areas with a heavier brush (see *Fig. 5–14*).

41

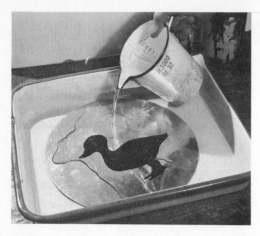

5–15

gloves and apron. Avoid any contact with skin or clothes; rinse and flush off with large amounts of water if an accident occurs.

A porcelain enameled tray (*Fig. 5–15*) or kitchen pan works well. For least amount of solution, place the aluminum part to be etched over a piece of heavy-duty aluminum foil and turn up foil edges all around to confine solution. Cover the aluminum surface with the etching solution. Pour the solution off after "boiling" stops . . . . 15 to 60 minutes. For a deeper etch, repeat the process.

Etch with a 50-50 mixture of muriatic acid and water. *Always* pour the *acid* into the *water*. Mix and store only in glass or crockery. Use a strong lye solution if acid is not available. Always wear rubber

After etching, rinse thoroughly with water. Remove blocking with a soft cloth soaked in turpentine, benzine, or kerosene. Be careful to avoid scratching the highly polished areas. Repolish with 000 steel wool and powdered pumice.

Chapter 6 . . .

PROJECTS FOR THE WORKSHOP

Sawhorse (*Fig. 6–1*) requires four 2′ lengths of 1¼″ aluminum tube for the legs. The top piece is a 3′ length of 2 x 4. Crosspieces are 10″ lengths of 2 x 4 fastened to the top piece 3″ in from each end. Use two ¼″ carriage bolts, 3½″ or longer for each crosspiece. Recess the heads down ¼″ from the top surface. Drill bolt holes on center line of the top piece 2½″ apart, providing ample clearance for the 1¼″ legs.

For drilling the leg holes, position the assembly under the drill by clamping to a 30° fixture as in *Fig. 4–56*. Cut the 30° blocks for this fixture using the miter gauge and setup in *Fig. 4–55*.

Figure 6–2 shows dimensions for drilling. Start leg holes 3⅛″ in from each end and center widthwise. Set depth stop to limit drill travel to about ¾″ into the top piece. Holes should just meet.

Insert tube into wood per instructions accompanying *Fig. 4–56*. Lock tube in place with a finishing nail. Set completed sawhorse on table top or level floor, and make all four feet touch simultaneously by trimming the longest leg as needed. Add white rubber crutch tips to give sawhorse firm footing.

Extension Switch Rod: A convenient way to operate the "on-off" switch on your power tools is to bring this control to the front of the machine by means of an extension rod like that on the drill press (*Fig. 6–3*). Set the toggle switch on the motor so that a forward pull turns it on, a push backward shuts it off.

If the arm of the switch does not have a hole in it, flatten the arm out with a hammer and drill a ³⁄₃₂″ diameter hole through the outer end of the arm. Now

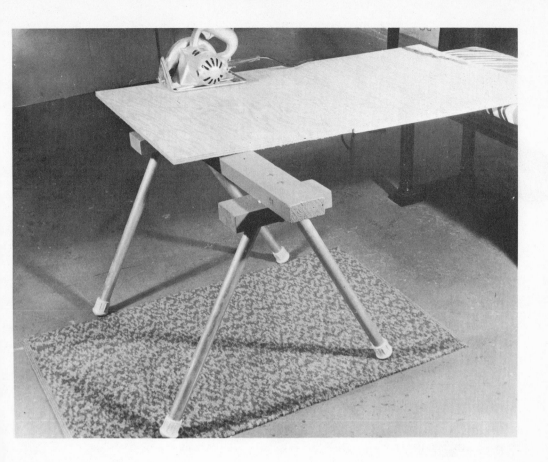

taper a piece of aluminum clothesline wire so that it can be hooked through the arm as in *Fig. 6–3.*

Make a guide bracket from $\frac{1}{8}$" x $\frac{3}{4}$" aluminum bar stock, and fasten it to any convenient part of the machine. Form a loop at the outer end to support the

6–2

switch rod. Curl up the front end of the switch rod to make a handy finger grip.

Now a short pull on the rod turns on the motor, a slight push shuts it off . . . . from the front of the tool where it is most convenient to operate. Such an extension switch rod will make almost any power tool easier to use.

6–3

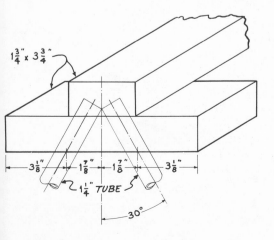

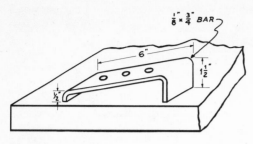

6–4

DEPTH STOP FOR PORTABLE DRILL: Often it is desirable to predetermine depth of holes accurately when using a portable electric drill. The handy depth stop shown in *Fig. 6–4* consists of an 8″ length of ⅛″ x ¾″ aluminum bar with the two legs bent as shown. Three ³⁄₁₆″ diameter holes drilled through the top section provide heights ranging from about ½″ to 1½″ above the work surface.

To use the depth stop, determine depth of hole desired. Insert wire drill of cor-rect size into the chuck of the tool, and put it through one of the holes in the depth stop. Adjust length of drill pro-truding from chuck so that drill extends from chuck through the depth stop and on to the depth desired.

To drill deep holes, use the ½″ end of the stop. For short holes, use the 1½″ end; for medium holes, the center. Cut longer or shorter legs on the depth stop where your particular work requirements dictate.

TOOL RACKS (*Fig. 6–5*) made from ¼″ x 1″ bar stock are particularly useful, as they are easily adapted to hold a wide variety of tools. Take a 4′ x 8′ panel of perforated Masonite nailed or screwed to a ½″ or ¾″ plywood panel backing. Seal Masonite panel with shellac, and paint with white enamel. Mount under ceiling trim strip as shown in *Fig. 6–6*.

6–5

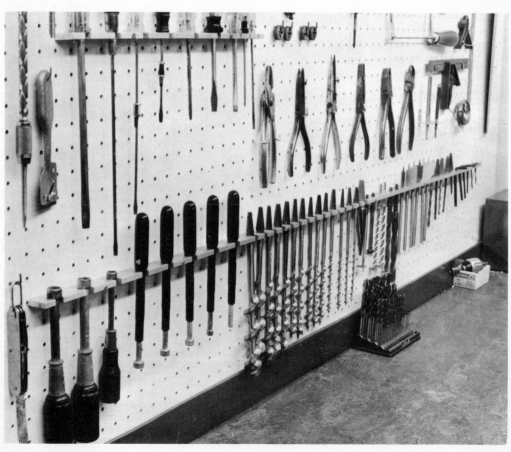

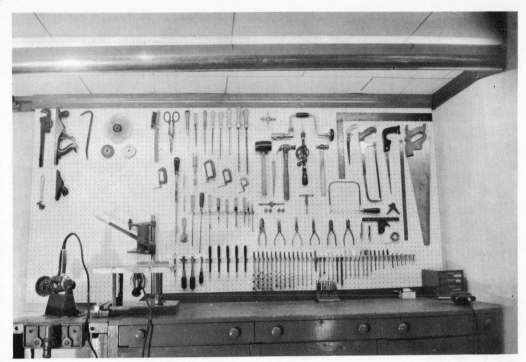

Racks for screwdrivers, socket wrenches, drills, and many other items are made from the 1″ bar stock by drilling a hole of size required by the tool and then making saw cuts from the front edge of bar to the holes. Mount bar edgewise to the panel by drilling clearance holes for 2″ long finishing nails. Clamp the bar in a vise so you are drilling upward at an angle (see *Fig. 2–14*). This allows gravity to help remove chips and prevent their becoming jammed at the bottom of hole. Lubricate also.

FLUORESCENT OVERHEAD LIGHTING: Workshop lighting can be from the ceiling, as in *Fig. 6–6*, or just above the workbench and storage shelves, as in *Fig. 6–7*. A piece of half-round aluminum eaves trough forms lighting fixture and reflector. Each of the units pictured houses two 40-watt fluorescent lamps, ballasts, and starters.

6–7

If ballasts are mounted on the outside of fixture, cut the trough 8'3" long; if mounted inside, cut the trough 11'1" long. Attach friction-type end caps, and lock with sheet-metal screws.

Bolt lamp sockets and starters to the inside of trough, as in *Fig. 6–8.* Connect with single-conductor insulated #14 fixture wire. There are two terminals on each socket and a socket for both ends of each lamp. Wiring is as follows: One side of the 110-volt line goes directly to either

6–8

terminal of one socket. Connect the other terminal of this same socket to one terminal of the starter. Connect the other terminal of starter to one terminal of the socket at the other end of lamp. Connect the other terminal of this socket to one terminal on the ballast. Connect the other

terminal on the ballast to one terminal of the pull-chain switch. The other terminal of the switch goes to the 110-volt line.

Fixtures are mounted with brackets made from ⅛" x ¾" bar bent as desired. When riveted to center of end cap (*Fig. 6–8*), the lamp fixture can be tilted downward for direct lighting as in *Fig. 6–7* or upward for indirect lighting where that is preferred.

TOOLBOXES: An ordinary small toolbox is made with 1/16" x 1" x 1" angle. First make bottom frame 9" x 18", and cut a ¼" plywood panel to fit it for reinforcing bottom. Bend corners per *Fig. 4–37.* Make lower box section from a single piece of embossed sheet, 27" x 36" and cut 9" x 9" squares from the four corners per *Fig. 3–7.* Put ½" hem on all four outside edges. Bend up around bottom frame, and rivet through angle and plywood panel. Set second frame 1" below top edge of box, per *Fig. 4–51,* to support tray. Cut four 8½" lengths of 1/16" x 1" x 1" angle for the vertical corner posts, position them on the outside, and rivet to the two frames. Make tray per *Figs. 9–2, 9–3, 9–4* and *9–5.*

The cover is another box section made without the angle frame but with corners locked, per *Fig. 4–7,* and with edges hemmed. Rivet ⅛" x ¾" bar around the inside of edge of cover for attaching hinges and latch. Fit a ¼" plywood panel inside top, and bolt through it to the handle of bent ⅛" bar.

Chapter 7 . . .

PROJECTS FOR THE KITCHEN

SHOPPING CART (*Fig. 7–1*) is 12″ across the front and 12″ on a side so a single sheet of perforated aluminum makes the front and both sides. The cart proper is 22½″ high. Thus a single sheet of plain aluminum is large enough to extend the length of the back, across the bottom, and up to form a flange at the front. Other edges of this sheet are flanged for riveting to the perforated metal.

The top is reinforced by ¾″ bar riveted on the outside of the sheet. Its two ends butt against the handle in back. A 14″ piece cut from a 6′ length of 1″ bar reinforces the top at the back on the inside. The remainder of the 1″ bar forms the

47

handle, extending down the back, across the bottom, and out in front to support the cart upright as shown in *Fig. 7–1*. A bicycle handlebar grip is cemented to the handle.

The small wheels are from your neighborhood cycle shop. The axle is attached to the cart with straps of ¾″ aluminum bar. The 1″ bar for the handle also passes around the axle to help support it.

STOVE VENT HOOD (*Fig. 7–2*) measures 3′ across the front and 2′ deep for the most economical use of material. At the top, the hood is 18″ wide and extends 12″ out from wall. Vary these dimensions for large or small stove tops. Sloping front and sides of plain or embossed aluminum measure 36″ from bottom to top. Front, sides, and top are framed with 1″ aluminum angle. To fit the frame, this angle is flattened out to form an angle greater than 90° by the method shown in *Fig. 3–22*.

One-inch bar reinforces the bottom edge all around. Rivet or bolt the assembly.

STOVE BACK BOARD (*Fig. 7–3*) employs embossed sheet. Aluminum trim strip finishes off the edges. Drill the trim strip at 6″ intervals for attaching to wall; then

se these holes as a guide to drill through
luminum sheet and plaster. See instruc-
ions accompanying *Fig. 4–3* for installing
heet-metal screws in plaster.

Figure 7–2 shows another style of finishing off a stove back board. Here the craftsman used plain sheet and framed it with
1" bar, matching the vent hood.

WINDOW-SILL COVER (*Fig.* 7–4) does not chip or show water or hot-dish marks because it is made of embossed aluminum. Cut a newspaper pattern to fit your particular window sill, extending over the front edge and under as pictured. Paste this pattern on the aluminum sheet, and cut it out with shears. Nail, cement, or screw the sheet in place.

If two pieces are needed to get the length required, join them as in *Fig.* 4–5 and accompanying instructions. Form the cover over the front of the sill with a rubber mallet. Then bend the front under, and tack it in place.

SINK WORK TOP (*Fig.* 7–5), made from plain aluminum sheet, is edged in front with aluminum trim strip. The work top and back shield are made in one piece; the end from another piece. All are cemented in place to avoid any tendency toward "oil-canning" effects. Follow cementing instructions at end of Chap. 4.

RADIATOR HEAT REFLECTOR (*Fig.* 7–6) employs an embossed aluminum sheet formed and attached to the wall with self-tapping sheet-metal screws as shown. See

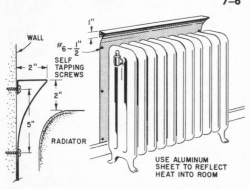

7–6

USE ALUMINUM SHEET TO REFLECT HEAT INTO ROOM

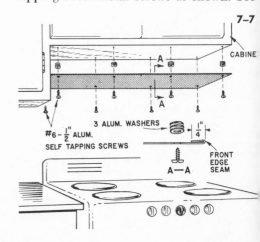

7–7

instructions for installing sheet-metal screws in plaster accompanying *Fig. 4–3.* Cut width and height to fit your radiator. Aluminum makes an excellent heat reflector.

CUPBOARD HEAT REFLECTOR (*Fig. 7–7*) prevents heat from stove top from damaging finish of cabinets mounted overhead. Cut a piece of embossed aluminum to fit your cabinet, plus 1/4″ for turning up a fold at the front to stiffen this edge. Mount to bottom of cabinet with washers between to form an air space as shown.

UTILITY TRAY (*Fig. 7–8*) is screwed to inside of sink cabinet panel and uses the space generally wasted between the back of this panel and the sink. It easily accommodates soap, dishcloth, cleaning brushes, and associated items. Lay out pattern (*Fig. 7–9*) on plain sheet, length according to panel space available.

Bend as shown in *Fig. 7–10*, and attach to front panel, which has been loosened from or cut out of sink front. Attach hinges along bottom edge with center line of hinge pins flush with front of panel. Trim top edge of panel to clear opening if necessary. Attach a short length of chain to hold panel when open.

HOT-DISH SERVER (*Fig. 7–11*) is a compact but highly useful item for bringing food and dishes from the kitchen to the dining room. Make three frames of 1/16″ x 1″ x 1″ angle, each 22″ long, but 8″, 12″, and 18″ wide, respectively. Notch and bend corners per *Fig. 4–37.* Upper two frames can

7–9

2 1/2″
1/4″
2″ R
1″
1″ R
1/2″
1/4″
2″   1″   2 1/2″

7–10

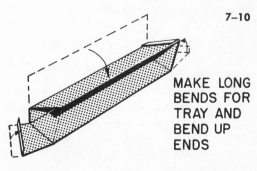

MAKE LONG BENDS FOR TRAY AND BEND UP ENDS

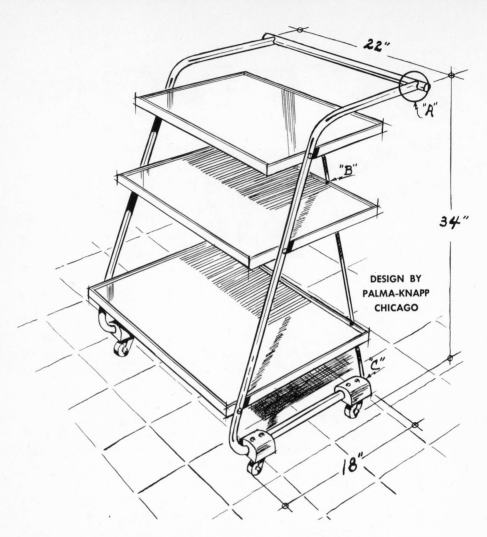

22"

"A"

"B"

34"

DESIGN BY
PALMA-KNAPP
CHICAGO

"C"

18"

be made from a single piece of angle 6' long. Use splice plates to join ends of frame pieces. Bottom frame requires splicing in an additional section at the back side.

Cut a panel of ½" plywood to fit inside bottom frame, and attach with screws up through angle into bottom of panel. Upper two frames can be used with glass or wood. Use 1" tube for ends, bending up at 60° angle 18" from bottom on 8" or 10" radius and another 60° angle for the handle as shown in *Fig. 7–11*. See *Fig. 4–64* for A-connection to handle.

Back support is a single piece of ⅜" rod bent into an A-frame, riveted to back edge of the panel frames at "B," and screwed to back end of foot block at "C." These foot blocks are a 4" length of 2 x 4

with a 1" hole to accommodate the tube frame. Regular casters are also set in these blocks, making the server handy to move around in any direction.

SERVING CART (*Fig. 7–12*) has ¾" plywood serving top 17" x 21". Box of ¾" plywood is 12" high at front end, 15" high at back end, 26" long front to back, 18" wide, outside dimensions, with sides open and a hole in the top 12½" wide, 10" long to fit the ice well made of plain sheet. This well is 14¼" high, 12" wide, 12" long at top, sloping to 8" long at bottom. To make watertight, seal edge with solder or aluminum mastic compound.

Note crossbar on handle with hooks for hanging cups. Rubber bumpers on bottom of box support the ice well and pre

ent it from scratching. An 8″-square
sheet of plain aluminum on top provides
surface for hot dishes. Finish as in *Fig.
–3*, and cement to wood top. Use 6″
diameter rubber-tired wheels from your
nearest cycle shop. See *Fig. 4–20* for end-
riveting of crossbar on handle and for the
bottom of the tripod-type legs. The ³⁄₈″
rod ends are bent parallel to wood surface and attached to wood box and serving top with round-head wood screws as
on front panel (*Fig. 7–12*).

SERVING TABLE (*Fig. 7–13*) employs simple construction. Make top frame of ¹⁄₁₆″
x 1″ x 1″ angle 23″ wide, 39″ long over
all, including 7½″ extension to handle
per *Fig. 7–14*. This allows for a double-
weight glass top 22¼″ x 31¼″ and the
bottle well 23″ long, 4″ deep, 3″ wide. A

7–12

7–13

53

22¼"   31¼"

7–14

flange 1″ high is bent out toward the handle to stiffen that edge and provide means for riveting to side frame members. Handle is ¾″ tube joined to angle as in *Fig. 4–68.*

From 1″ tube, cut two back legs 42″ long and two front legs 38″ long. Join to top frame as in *Fig. 4–60.* Wheels are ¾″ plywood, 8″ in diameter (see *Fig. 4–84*). Drill hole where legs cross 21″ from top end of each, and bolt before attaching to top frame.

The V-shelf is embossed sheet 18″ x 24″. Put a 1″ hem (*Fig. 3–5*) along each 24″ side. Make a 90° bend in center of sheet lengthwise. Attach to legs with sheet-metal self-tapping screws. This shelf stiffens the structure; so use enough screws or bolts to assure solid connections. Spacer bar between back legs is ⅜″ rod 9″ from leg ends, end-riveted per *Fig. 4–21.*

UTILITY STAND (*Fig. 7–15*) has four shelves of ¾″ plywood cut to the same size. The unit pictured was made to fit an electric roaster, employing the same radius of corner curvature as the roaster. The top of each shelf is protected with a sheet of plain aluminum, cemented in

position, per instructions at the end of Chap. 4. Trim aluminum sheets to exact size and contour of shelf. Add the edge trim to each shelf.

Next drill four ¾″ diameter holes 2½″ in from edge and side of each of the three lower shelves. Wobble drill slightly after it emerges through the shelf to provide clearance in assembling tubes. Drill top shelf only ⅝″ deep from under side. To assemble the ¾″ tube legs into the shelves, position top shelf upside down on a mat or thin rug on the floor. Then drive the four legs into the top shelf.

Lubricate tube thoroughly with paraffin or an old candle. Now position second shelf on legs and drive down into place, using a rubber mallet or a wood scrap to protect shelf during hammering. Drive third and fourth shelves into position in same manner.

Lock shelves in position by driving finishing nails through edge of shelf and into each of the four legs.

7–15

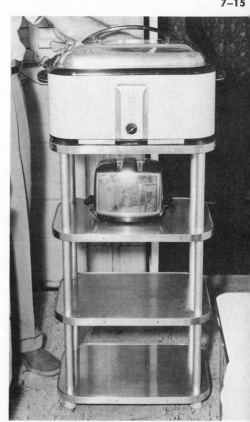

Chapter 8 . . .

PROJECTS FOR THE DINING ROOM

DINING-ROOM TABLE (CONFERENCE TABLE):
With the color scheme suggested, the
table shown in *Fig. 8–1* presents an exceptionally bright, highly modern appearance. The table top proper consists of two
¾″ thick sheets of plywood. Use pine
Nov-A-Ply for the top sheet, and trim with
side rails of maple, stained cherry red.

8–2

FOUR 3½″ FLAT HEAD
WOOD SCREWS

FOUR 2″ FINISHING NAILS

2″

1¼″ ⌀ HOLE 7° FROM
VERTICAL

THREE ¾″ PLYWOOD (FIR)
BLOCKS, 4″x 7″

Inset the outer edge with ¼″ x 1″ aluminum bar.

While it is easy to make this table in
any size up to 4′ x 8′, the 3′ x 5′ size (for
six people) or the 42″ x 6′ size (for eight
people) is best for most dining rooms.
The 3′ x 6′ size makes an excellent conference table.

Since side and end rails are 1¼″ thick,
cut the two panels 2½″ shorter and narrower than over-all dimensions selected.
Place the two panels upside down, and
screw them together from the "underside," using flat-head wood screws 1¼″
long in a line 4″ in from the outside edges
and spaced on 6″ centers. Put a final row
down center of the panels lengthwise.

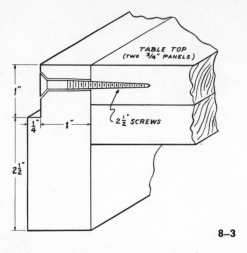

TABLE TOP
(TWO 3/4" PANELS)

1"

1/4"

1"

2 1/2" SCREWS

2 1/2"

8–3

Two 1¼″ diameter aluminum tubes are used for legs at each corner of the table. So make eight plywood blocks (*Fig. 8–2*). Drill them to fit the tubes, making the holes 7° from the vertical, using angle block and setup pictured in *Fig. 4–57*. Assemble 36″ lengths of tube into these blocks as directed in instructions accompanying *Fig. 4–57*. With blocks on level surface, make horizontal cut on legs to provide vertical height of 29″. This, plus the 1½″ thickness of the two panels, makes the table surface 30½″ from the floor. This height allows most chair arms to easily clear the bottom of the side rails which are 3½″ deep.

Make alignment jig per *Fig. 4–58* and accompanying instructions. Use it to position the legs. Secure the blocks to the underside of the table while it is still upside down on the floor. Use 3½″ flat-head wood screws. Drill and countersink holes for them in the blocks before positioning blocks. Use these clearance holes to mark for drilling pilot holes in table top.

Drill pilot holes only 1″ or 1¼″ deep. Use the depth stop (*Fig. 6–4*) with a portable electric drill to avoid drilling too deeply.

Now reposition the blocks, and drive the 3½″ screws, using a hand brace fitted with a screwdriver bit, instead of a screwdriver. Then join each pair of legs together at the tip with an aluminum bolt, drilling down through open end of one

leg. File leg tips to remove burrs and sharp edges.

With legs anchored to table, turn table right side up for attaching side and end rails and for finishing. Side rails are 1¼ x 3½″ pieces of maple, which must be absolutely straight and true to make the assembly go together properly. If you have any doubts about being able to purchase such items, buy them oversize and cut down to exact dimensions yourself on a jointer to make them straight and true.

Next, cut out upper corner of rails to take the aluminum bar. Make a 1″ deep cut first, with saw fence adjusted to make cut exactly ¼″ from outside surface of rail. Then make the ¼″ deep cut with fence set to cut exactly 1″ from top of rail. Use scrap pieces of wood to check these settings before cutting rails.

Before mounting rails, go over edges of table panels with a belt sander to make them absolutely straight and true. Be especially careful of the top outer edge. Panel edges must be exactly 90° with table surface.

Now cut rails to exact over-all length required to fit sides and ends of table top, with 45° miters at corners. Mount rails with 2½″ flat-head screws on 6″ centers *into the top panel*, as indicated in *Fig. 8–3*. Drill clearance holes in rail and countersink so screwheads come below rail surface. Mount rails in correct position, and clamp with large C-clamps across table top. Then drill pilot holes into panel edge, using clearance holes as a guide. Now drive the screws.

Cut ¼″ x 1″ aluminum bar to length required. Do not miter bar joints at table corners. Instead, lap the side bars over the end bars at corners. Before applying end bars, bow center outward slightly. Then a single screw at the center will hold the entire bar snugly in position.

Side bars require three screws each, one about 8″ to 10″ in from each end and another in the middle. After drilling holes in the bars, glue bars in position. Hold with C-clamps across table top. Bars are also anchored mechanically with 1

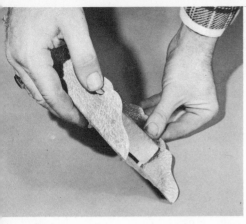

8–4

flat-head aluminum screws. When countersunk, filed smooth, and finished according to *Fig. 4–32* and accompanying directions, screws will blend with bar and not be visible.

Recommended sequence of finishing operations is: Sand the Nov-A-Ply table surface perfectly smooth and level. Seal by brushing on two thin coats of transparent wipe-on type "plastic finish." Stain and seal side and end rails. Then assemble to table. Install bar edging. Fin-

ish entire table with two coats of transparent wipe-on type plastic finish, wiping on heavy coats. Rub lightly between coats. Result will be clear, glasslike finish. Apply finish over aluminum bar as well as wood surfaces. Clean the aluminum thoroughly with fine steel wool, rubbing in lengthwise direction only, before applying finish. Be careful to avoid finger-marking the aluminum.

Clean and brighten the aluminum legs by rubbing lengthwise with fine steel wool. To retain brilliance and avoid finger marking here, apply light coat of paste wax and polish with clean dry cloth.

GADGET SHELF (*Fig. 8–4*) is made from embossed sheet, using your own design ideas for outline. Size depends upon space you have available. Unit shown is 6″ wide, 6″ high, 2″ deep, with two shelves. Back and two sides are of one piece of sheet, with sides bent up 90°. Each shelf is a separate piece of sheet cut to width desired and here about 1½″ deep with a ½″ flange turned up at front edge.

No bolts or rivets are used, as slots and

8–5

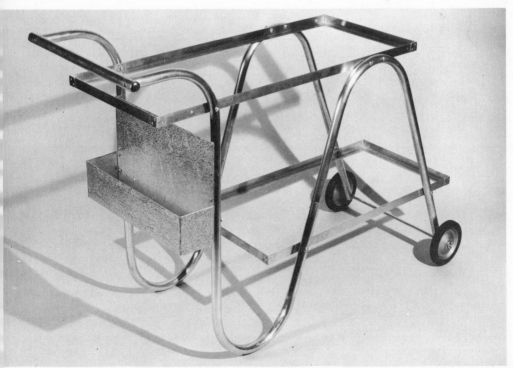

ears hold the shelves in place. Make ears about 1/4″ wide and 1/4″ long; round off corners. Cut slots with screwdriver blade and hammer on hardwood block. Assemble by inserting ears in matching slots and bending over (see *Fig. 4–4*).

SERVING CART (*Fig. 8–5*) is an exceptionally useful item. Frames for both upper and lower glass shelves are made from 1/8″ x 3/4″ x 3/4″ angle. Top frame is 36″ long; bottom 30″. Both are 18″ wide. Cut and miter corners. Use riveted outside splice plates for corner joints (*Fig. 4–35*). Bend the 3/4″ tube framing on 9″ radii per *Fig. 3–27* and accompanying instructions. Two pieces of tube go into each side frame, the two pieces being joined end to end with wood dowel rod per *Fig. 4–63*. Join tube and angle members with through bolts.

For bottle holder, cut and bend up a sheet of embossed aluminum as in *Fig. 8–6*. First cut out the 1/2″ square corners shown solid. Then fold 180° the flanges numbered 1, 2, 3, 4, and 5. Then make 90° bends at 6, 7, and 8. Flanges 1, 2, and 3 are folded back; flanges 4 and 5 folded up. Make bends 6, 7, and 8 in the "up" direction, also.

Obtain wheels at local cycle shop or make them from plywood. Attach with 3/8″ rod, per *Fig. 4–84*. For the glass shelves, use double-weight window glass. Cover edges with clear Scotch tape by centering tape strip over edge, pressing

down equal amounts on each side of glass. Use two layers of tape to provide proper cushion for glass.

8–7

STORAGE TABLE (*Fig. 8–7*) is 30″ high, 15″ front to back, with lower shelf 8″ above floor and upper box section 9″ deep. Of course, these dimensions can be varied as you wish. Use 1/8″ x 3/4″ x 3/4″ angle for the four legs. That is all the aluminum necessary, unless you wish to use two additional pieces of the 3/4″ angle as stretchers between the legs to hold the shelf at each end. In this case, cut stretchers and rivet to legs at corners. Remainder of table is 3/4″ plywood. Make sliding doors per *Fig. 4–82*.

Make and assemble table box section first. Then screw legs to box and rivet legs to stretchers (if used). Fit shelf in place. Attach handles to doors, and insert sliding doors in travel slots.

COLLAPSIBLE TABLE (*Fig. 8–8*) has top of 3/4″ plywood, edge trimmed with 1/16″ x 1″ x 1″ angle per *Fig. 4–50*. Use 1″ tube for the legs. Hinge legs at top by bolting to 3″ T-type hinges set 45° into each corner so legs will fold toward center of table. Corner braces are 3/8″ rod cut 36″ long. Bend rod on 1″ radius in exact center as shown in *Fig. 8–8*. Bend a 2″ length at right angles on each end to swivel against underside of table top. Fasten to table top

8–6

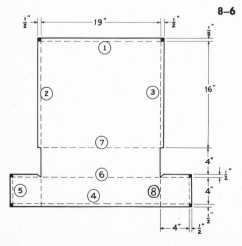

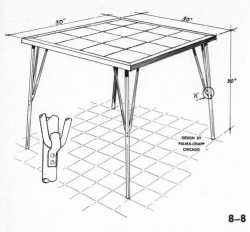

30" 30"
30"
"A"

8–8

with straps made of 3" lengths of 1/8" x 3/4" bar placed crosswise the rod ends. This allows rod braces to fold against underside of table.

Note close-up "A" of rod brace to tube-leg connection made with 3" length of 1/8" x 3/4" bar, shaped as shown and fastened to leg with self-tapping screws or through bolts.

BAR OR SERVER (*Fig. 8–9*) is a design that will be found most easy to construct. Upper "box" section of 1/2" plywood is 12" high with interior divided into two shelves for 16" of its length. Bottom shelf here is 10" deep. Note that face slopes to match slope of front legs.

Lower "box" section of 3/4" plywood is 16" deep, same length as upper section, 26", and 14" high, with sliding Masonite doors, per *Fig. 4–82*. A perforated Mason-ite panel between the two box sections

8–9

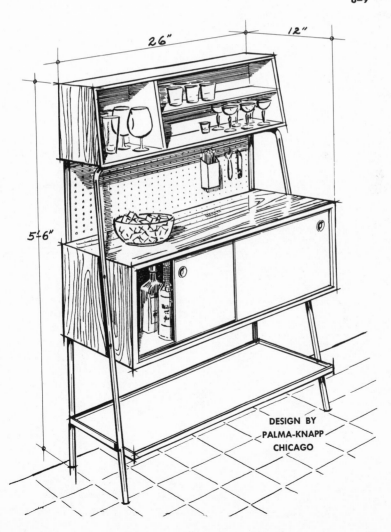

26" 12"

5–6"

offers a means for hanging can and bottle openers, ice pick, straws, and mixer sticks.

Cut back legs 64″ long. Place lower box section face down on floor (pad to avoid marring). Position back legs 2″ in from ends and so top of box will be 30″ above floor when unit is set upright. Bolt through tubes to back of box section to attach legs. Now attach upper box section in a similar manner. Position so top of legs will be 2″ below top of box when upright.

Next cut perforated Masonite panel to fit between back legs and lap over both boxes at least 1″, and screw to boxes. At this point, turn entire assembly over so back of boxes is toward floor. Now cut and fit front legs as shown in *Fig. 8–9*. Note that upper end of front legs extends under box section to which it is attached with bolts. See tube-bending instructions accompanying *Fig. 3–27*.

Construct lower shelf frame from $\frac{1}{16}$″ x 1″ x 1″ angle to outside measurements of 26″ x 14″, with corners per *Fig. 4–37*.

Use a single 8′ length of angle, or splice in a piece in the back if 6′ length is used. Cut and fit shelf of double-weight window glass, covering edges of glass with clear Scotch tape before inserting in frame to avoid glass-to-metal contact.

PLANTER, at rear in *Fig. 8–10*, is 14″ long, 4″ wide, 2″ deep, with $\frac{3}{4}$″ diameter curls around all four top edges. Make from a single plain sheet, 21″ long, 11″ wide, notched in $3\frac{1}{2}$″ at each corner, as shown in *Fig. 3–7* for making box sections. Cut sheet and notch it; then make curls (*Fig. 3–11*) and finally the 90° bends. Corners are not locked but left open. Planter is made waterproof by using a piece of heavy-duty aluminum foil as a liner.

Planter legs are in pairs, each pair a U-shaped piece made by curling down each end of a 4″ x 8″ piece of plain sheet. Rivet to bottom of planter. Polish with steel wool, and apply wax or lacquer.

ASH-TRAY SET, at extreme right in *Fig.*

8–10

8–10, consists of six 3″ diameter circles cut from plain sheet, grained in sections per *Fig. 5–8*. Then form scallops around edge as in *Fig. 3–9*. Flower designs are easily scratched or etched into the surface. See Chap. 5 on Surface Finishes. The holder for the tray set is made like the trays except that ½″ x 1½″ ears are left opposite each other, then curled up to form clips.

CANDY-DISH SET, foreground in *Fig. 8–10*, consists of three pieces. The tray underneath the other two is a single piece of plain sheet 8″ wide, 16″ long. The 2½″ on each end is cut down to form a ¾″ diameter curl 3½″ long (see *Fig. 3–11*).

Cut remainder of material to an oval outline, and put three large scallops into each edge as shown.

Cut each of the two smaller dishes from a 6″ x 7½″ piece of plain sheet. Lay out a 6″ diameter circle on one end, and reduce the other end from 6″ down to 5″ by making two lines each ½″ in from the side, up to meet the circle. Cut this outline, grain the circle in sections (per *Fig. 5–8*), and curl up the other end to meet the circle, using a ¾″ dowel rod.

NAPKIN RINGS, left foreground in *Fig. 8–10*, are simply 2″ x 8″ pieces of plain or embossed sheet formed to an oval and initialed if desired.

Chapter 9 . . .

PROJECTS FOR THE BEDROOM

RODS FOR CLOTHES CLOSET (*Fig. 9–1*) are made from 1¼″ tube cut to exact distance from wall to wall minus ¼″ for clearance. Two 1″ thick wood blocks, 4″ square and screwed to wall, support the tube. Cut 1½″ diameter hole in one block and 1½″ U-shaped opening in the other to permit insertion and removal of the rod (see *Fig. 4–78*). Be sure to locate blocks over studs in the wall.

9–1

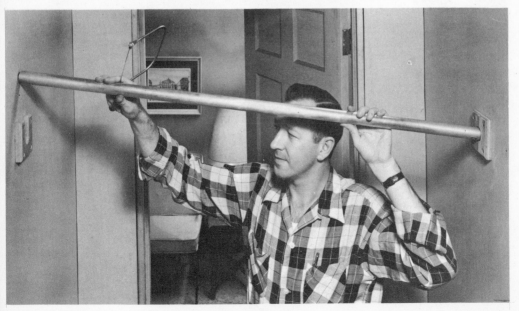

SLIDING TRAY FOR DRAWER (*Fig. 9–2*) utilizes space ordinarily wasted in top of drawers in chests and dressing tables. The metal tray is 1″ deep and quickly slides out of the way or lifts free from angle slides.

To make tray, cut a piece of sheet 12″ wide and length determined as follows: Measure depth of drawer (from inside front to inside back). Add 2″ for each partition desired; add another 3″ for making the ends; subtract ¼″ to provide sliding clearance.

Mark location of partitions, and make 180° bends at those points by clamping and bending as in *Fig. 9–3*. Change clamps, and make the 90° bends as in *Fig. 9–4*. Form the ends by bending a ½″ fold first and then making the 90° bend. With tray forming completed, assemble it to 1/16″ x 1″ x 1″ angle by riveting (*Fig. 9–5*). These sides are cut the same length as the distance from inside front to inside back of drawer minus ¼″ for clearance.

To make slides for the tray, cut two pieces of 1/16″ x 1″ x 1″ angle the same length as width of drawer. Saw one leg off so that it is only ⅜″ wide instead of 1″, and mount against inside of drawer front

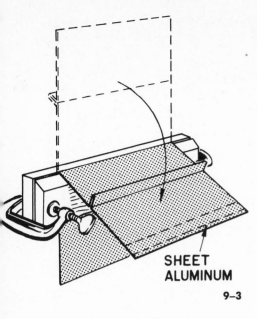

SHEET
ALUMINUM

9–3

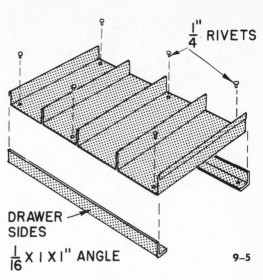

$\frac{1}{4}$" RIVETS

DRAWER
SIDES

$\frac{1}{16}$ X I X I" ANGLE

9–5

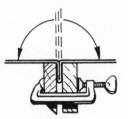

9–4

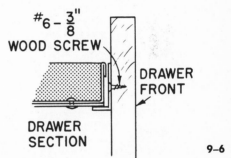

#6 – $\frac{3}{8}$"
WOOD SCREW

DRAWER
FRONT

DRAWER
SECTION

9–6

9–7

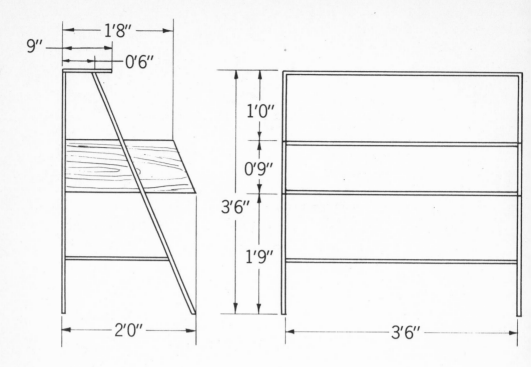

about 2″ below top edge of drawer sides as shown in *Fig. 9–2*. Attach other slide against inside of drawer back, 2″ down also. Countersink and mount with screwheads flush as detailed in *Fig. 9–6*.

VANITY TABLE (*Fig. 9–7*) has frame made from 1/8″ x 3/4″ x 3/4″ angle with flat surfaces of 3/4″ plywood. The angle-to-angle joints are all riveted except where the upper end of the back leg is bent forward (see *Fig. 4–39*) to form a support for the top shelf. Or a separate piece of angle may be turned over and riveted to the back leg to support the top shelf similar to *Fig. 4–74*. Countersink wood screws flush with angle surface.

The only trick here is to saw a 3/16″ wide slot in each end of the box section to take the front leg as it comes up past the box. Don't make this cut until you have assembled the frame, fitted the box into it, and marked the cut directly from the frame itself. See *Figs. 4–53* and *4–54* for details. Dimensions are on *Fig. 9–8*.

The simplicity of this design is its high point. Back panel of box provides length-wise rigidity. End panels provide front-to-back rigidity.

SEWING TABLE (*Fig. 9–9*) uses a flush door measuring 2½′ x 6′ for the top. Shelves are 3/4″ plywood cut 15″ x 24″. Legs and stretchers are 1/8″ x 3/4″ x 3/4″ angle. Diagonal reinforcing members are 1/8″ x 3/4″ bar riveted to the leg angles as shown.

Cut legs 29½″ long to allow 3/4″ top and bottom for cutting away 3/4″ of one face to make flat (see *Fig. 4–49*) to prevent digging into the floor at the bottom and for connecting top end to underside of table as in *Fig. 4–47*.

Attach shelves to legs with screws through legs. Before running these screws up tight, cut and rivet the cross braces to the legs. Put a rivet through the braces where they cross each other. These braces provide the rigid frame structure required. A plywood panel (as thin as 1/4″) may also be used in place of the cross braces to stiffen the structure.

Next, turn table top upside down and attach legs. Now rivet the top front stretcher and the lower rear

9–9

stretcher in place. These, with the stretcher and cross brace between the right-hand legs, make the framework of the desk completely rigid. A plywood panel may be substituted for the brace and stretcher between the right-hand legs if desired.

Where additional shelf space is wanted, add another pair of shelves at the right-hand end of the desk. These shelves can easily be converted to cupboard or storage units merely by adding a door and enclosing sides and back. If sliding drawers are desired instead of shelves, attach drawer slides made from the ¾″ angle and riveted to the legs inside the corners as detailed in *Fig. 4–52.*

EARRING STORAGE (*Fig. 9–11*) is easy to build into any shallow drawer . . . . or

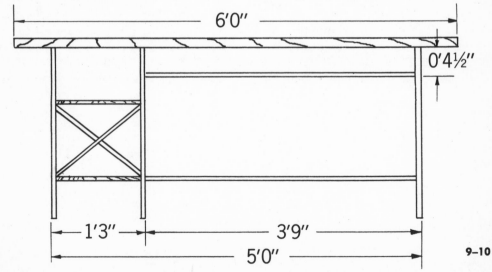

6'0″

0'4½″

1'3″

3'9″

5'0″

9–10

to mount in top part of a deeper drawer, like the unit shown in *Figs. 9–2* and *9–6*. The earrings are hung on vertical divider sections.

Cut a sheet of plain aluminum as wide as the drawer and the same length as the drawer plus 2″ for each vertical element to be used with button type earrings and 4″ for each one used with pendant type earrings. Then bend the sheet as shown in *Figs. 9–3* and *9–4* to make the same type structure shown in *Fig. 9–5*. This produces a 1″ high vertical element for button earrings, and 2″ high elements for pendant. Arrange the work so the 2″ high elements come at back of drawer.

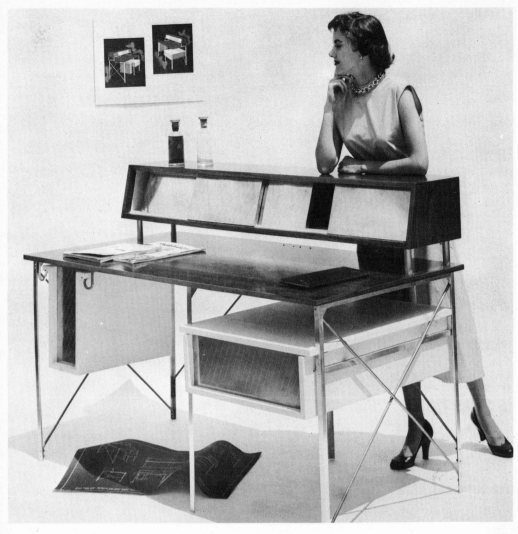

Chapter 10 . . .

PROJECTS FOR THE STUDY DEN

DESIGNER'S DESK (*Fig. 10–1*) is a high-style item with several novel features. Desk top itself is ¾″ plywood cut to 30″ x 60″. Six pieces of ⅛″ x ¾″ x ¾″ angle 29¼″ long make the legs. Rivet each pair to a top crosspiece of ¾″ angle 28½″ long. Use reinforcing splice plates at connections. Two 36″ pieces of ⅜″ rod are next riveted crosswise between each pair of legs for bracing. Flatten rod at end by

hammering, drill, and rivet.

Now turn table top upside down, and attach legs to underside of table top with wood screws. The center pair of legs are located 24″ from the right pair measured between outside faces. Attach 36″ pieces of ⅜″ rod to back corner legs and up to back edge of table top for lateral bracing. Turn entire structure right side up for completing.

Left-hand drawer is a box of ¾" plywood 6" wide, 14" high, and 18" deep, inside, and open at top. Front is closed with Masonite panel covered with plain aluminum sheet with the diamond scratch pattern of *Fig. 5–4.* Set this panel in slots cut 1" in from front of box. Drawer supports are ¾" x 1½" x 18" pieces attached to outside upper edges and riding on drawer slides made of ⅜" rod hanging down from underside of table top. Make drawer, install left-hand drawer slide, then position right-hand slide, using drawer as a guide.

The right-hand drawer sets just below a shelf of ¾" plywood 23½" wide, 30½" deep, fitted inside the angle frame by notching edges of shelf. Drawer is a ¾" plywood box 21½" wide, 7½" high, 30½" deep, outside dimensions, open at top. Front is closed the same as the other

drawer above. Drawer has a ⅜" deep slot cut in the outside surface of each side, 2" from top edge for engaging with drawer slide of ¾" angle riveted to the legs as per *Fig. 4–52.* Note that slots end 2" from front of drawer.

Upper section of desk is a ¾" plywood box 60" wide, 7½" high, 12" deep on bottom, 10" deep on top, outside dimensions, open in front, with ends and front faces of top and bottom sloped to match. Sliding doors are Masonite, each 13" long and covered with plain sheet per *Fig. 5–4.* See *Fig. 4–82* for sliding-door data. Two doors slide in front slots; two in back slots. This box sets on four legs of 1" tube filled with ¾" wood dowel rod. Set legs 2" in from edge of box. Attach with wood screws up through table top and down through box. For convenience, attach legs before putting top piece on box.

MAGAZINE TABLE (*Fig. 10–2*) is exceptionally easy to construct. Most people will prefer it about 60″ long, 18″ or 24″ wide, 22″ or 24″ high. Make table top of ¾″ plywood, doubled to 1½″ at edges by adding strips underneath around edge. Trim with ¹⁄₁₆″ x 1″ x 1″ angle added to top or inset in top per *Fig. 4–50*.

Suggested dimensions are 24″ wide, 12″ deep at bottom, 14″ high for top box; bottom box is the same depth as table width. It may be 16″ high, 24″ long. Legs are ⅜″ rod, riveted together at bottom left, and attached to wood with round-headed screws through the rod.

PORTABLE BAR OR TEA SERVICE (*Fig. 10–3*) is an ideal unit for the rumpus room. Top panel is ⅜″ or ½″ plywood or Nov-A-Ply, 16″ x 55″. A 6′ piece of ⅛″ x ¾″ x ¾″ angle frames the front and half of each end. Two pieces complete frame top. Bend corners per *Fig. 4–39*. Cupboard below is 14″ deep, 27″ wide, 14″ high, over all, made of ¾″ plywood with front edges covered with ¾″ angle frame and fitted with perforated Masonite sliding doors (*Fig. 4–82*) painted white.

The legs of ¾″ tube support serving top 30″ above floor by a unique system of spacers and ⅜″ rod braces that give this unit its novel appearance. Additional braces for front legs are recommended extending diagonally up underneath to bottom of cupboard. Rods are riveted to bottom of legs through open end of legs. See *Fig. 4–64* for details of tube-to-tube T-joint on back legs which are flattened at top and screwed to underside of serving top. Bend front legs per *Fig. 3–27* and accompanying instructions.

COCKTAIL TABLE (*Fig. 10–4*) is a delicate, highly modernistic design, 16″ wide, 18″ high, 42″ long. The center section is a 24″ x 16″ piece of lincane pattern perforated sheet (*Fig. 1–8*). The two end sections of the table top are 10″ x 16″ pieces of ½″ plywood finished in black enamel. Start construction by making the plywood panels and finishing them.

The 1/16″ x 1″ x 1″ angle used for the frame is made in two pieces, each extending down a side and halfway across each end. Bend the corners per *Fig. 4–37*. Fit the two butt joints to exactly 16″ inside dimensions across the end of the table. Position the perforated sheet in the center of frame, lay the two plywood panels

in position, screw the frame to underside of panels, and screw the perforated sheet to underside of panels.

For the handles and legs, take a 6′ length of ⅜″ rod; first form a 6″ handle by making a 90° bend 3″ each side of the center of the rod. Bend the rod under the table ends by making 90° bends as shown. At 6″ in under the table, bend the legs down and out toward the table corners as shown in *Fig. 10–4*. Turn table upside down on 2″ x 4″ blocks. Attach legs to underside of panels with straps formed from ⅛″ x ¾″ bar stock and screwed to panels. Now adjust the legs so that at a point 18″ from the table top, they come exactly over the table corners. Cut off legs at this point. Round them off, and turn completed table right side up. Polish aluminum with steel wool, and wax or lacquer.

STUDY DESK (*Fig. 10–5*) employs a cull door which is cut to 24″ x 48″ and open edges closed with wood to match the solid edges. Or a ¾″ thick piece of plywood may be used, doubled to 1½″ thickness by screwing ¾″ x 4″ strips underneath

10–5

around all four edges of the table top.

Left end panel (*Fig. 10–5*) is made by screwing two pieces of $\frac{1}{16}''$ x 1" x 1" angle cut 28" long to a $\frac{3}{4}''$ plywood panel 18" x 22". To keep ends of legs from digging into the floor, cut and bend 1" tips as shown in *Fig. 4–49*, or attach rubber bumpers (*Fig. 4–48*). Turn table top upside down. Secure end panel to the table top with two 8" shelf brackets screwed to inside of panel and to underside of table top. Position end panel 1" inside front and back edges of table top and $1\frac{1}{4}''$ in from table end.

For a plain table, make a second end panel, attach legs, and secure to table top at other end with another pair of shelf brackets.

For the double-shelf design (*Fig. 10–5*) make two end panels using $\frac{3}{4}''$ plywood sections measuring 12" x 22". Cut four pieces of 1" angle 29" long. Cut and bend at top and screw to underside of table top per *Fig. 4–47*. Cut and bend to close lower ends per *Fig. 4–48* or *4–49*. Before attaching legs to table top, screw panels to legs so panels will be 6" below table top.

Cut two pieces of plywood 20" x 22", and screw one above and the other below the two plywood sections just completed, to form the two shelves. Lateral support is provided by a $\frac{3}{4}''$ plywood panel $13\frac{1}{2}''$ x 20" screwed just inside the back edges of the four panels, closing the back end of the box. This panel is mounted inside the other panels in the box by screwing through these panels into the edge of the back panel.

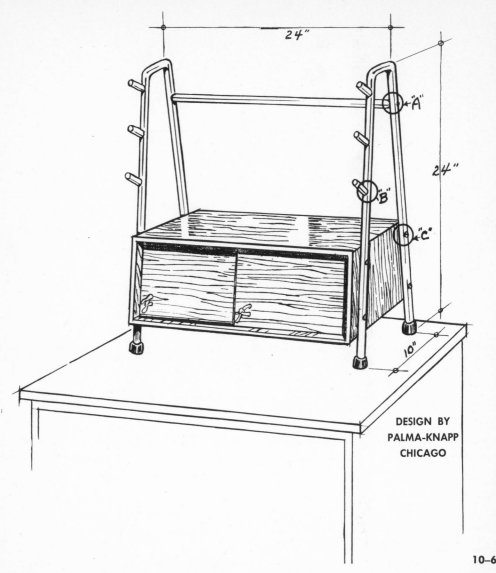

DESIGN BY
PALMA-KNAPP
CHICAGO

10-6

GUN RACK (*Fig. 10–6*) is an attractive item for any sportsman's den. Make the A-frames of ¾″ tube 4″ across the top, with legs 10″ apart at the bottom and with the back leg vertical. See *Fig. 3–27* and instructions on tube bending. Only the front leg slants. Make the box from ¾″ plywood to a width outside of 24″, 10″ high, 14″ deep at bottom. Slant front to match the A-frames. Install sliding doors per *Fig. 4–82* and accompanying instructions.

Put rubber crutch tips on bottom of legs, and bolt A-frames to ends of box as shown at "C." Add stretcher bar of ¾″ tube across back of legs 4″ from top of A-frames. Install dowel rod in ends, and

screw to back legs at "A" per *Fig. 4–64*.

Pins in front legs are also ¾″ tube, each 4″ long with wood dowel inserts for attaching to A-frames at right angles at "B," same as at "A." Locate top pin 2″ from top of A-frame. Other pins are 5″ apart center to center.

TYPEWRITER WORKTABLE (*Fig. 10–7*) has two panels on either end of ½″ plywood 12″ x 18″ bolted into frames of $\frac{1}{16}$″ x 1″ x 1″ angle. Each frame is a single piece of angle, with corners notched and bent as in *Fig. 4–37*. Each pair of legs is made from a single 6′ length of ¾″ tube bent into an inverted U 30″ on the side and 12″ across the top. See *Fig. 3–27* and ac-

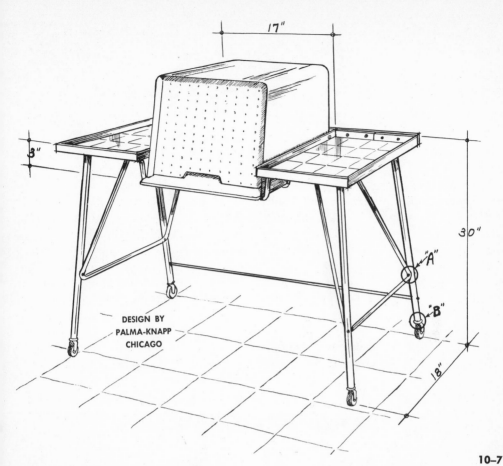

17"

3"

30"

"A"

"B"

DESIGN BY
PALMA-KNAPP
CHICAGO

18"

companying instructions on tube bending.

Center panel of ½″ plywood is 17″ x 18″. Typewriter cover is plain sheet fitted with ½″ plywood back and perforated Masonite front panels. Bracing uses two 5′ lengths of ⅜″ rod, one for each end panel of the table. Each brace extends 1″ under center panel, bends up 3″ to end panel, runs along underneath end panel for 4″, then extends 20″ down to leg across 16″ to other leg and back up.

Prepare parts above, and assemble as follows: Join top panels with 41″ length of ¼″ x 1″ bar bolted outside against the back ends of the two frames for the top panels. Fit panels, and bolt into frames. Now bolt each pair of legs to top panel, positioning legs 3″ inside the edge of panels and centered front to back. Next end-rivet a 40″ length of ⅜″ rod as a stretcher between the back legs 4″ above the floor, per *Fig. 4–21*. Bolt each set of braces in place under the end panels. At-

tach center panel to brace ends by using small straps of ⅛″ x ¾″ bar bent over the rod and screwed into underside of center panel. Complete structural framework by attaching braces to legs at "A," using pins made from aluminum nails. Add casters at "B," if you wish, by driving in dowel rods and fitting casters into dowels.

L-P Record Holder or Bookshelf (*Fig. 10–8*) is 30″ long or cut to fit your space. Make from ¾″ plywood and ⅛″ x ¾″ x ¾″ angle. The novel feature here is the front leg, made by notching and bending 24″ length of ¾″ angle. First notch and bend the back corner, per *Fig. 4–39*.

Now make a 45° saw cut in 3″ from the other end, per *Fig. 10–9*, and bend down as shown. Saw or file off top of this bent leg to come parallel with bottom of shelf and so bottom is parallel to table top. Secure to shelf bottom by flat-head screws

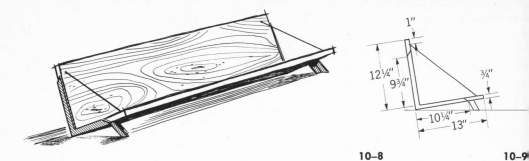

countersunk into underside of shelf.

Make book stops at each end with three lengths of picture wire or aluminum clothesline wire. Insert top wire 1" down, and space others 1" apart. Install wires 2" in from each end by drilling panels and tacking wire on opposite side.

MAGAZINE RACK (*Fig. 10–10*) utilizes two pieces of ⅜" rod each 42" long for the frame and a single piece of embossed sheet 12" x 30" for the container. Start forming the sheet by marking off a line 12" in from each end. Then cut a curve on each corner as shown and bend up a curl to wrap around the rod at each end, per *Fig. 3–11*. Then make 90° bends at the lines marked out, clamping the sheet as in *Fig. 3–6*.

Now make the two bends in each rod about 14" from each end, using a 4" to 6" radius, bending around a circular form

block to assure uniform shaping. Paint black, and let dry. Insert rods in sheet section, and close curls as tightly as possible. Trim corners of sheet if necessary to clear rods. Notch the rods deeply with a three-cornered file where they cross each other 6″ from end of rod. Also cut sharp notches on the outside of each rod at these same points. Now cross rods, engage notches, and secure tightly by wrapping with strong cord such as fish line, or use picture-frame wire. Apply two thin coats of shellac or Duco cement, or glue to wrapping to help secure rods. Cover joint with small piece of embossed sheet as in *Fig. 10–10*.

FLIGHT CAGE (*Fig. 10–11*) gives birds lots of room for flying. It measures 36″ long, 24″ high, and 18″ deep. Framing is $\frac{1}{16}$″ x 1″ x 1″ angle, cut and mitered at each corner, with the vertical corner posts acting as an inner strap joining the sections. See *Fig. 4–43* for corner details. The door is 12″ wide, centered in front face of cage.

Embossed sheet, 6″ high, is riveted around sides and ends of cage for a splash guard. Upper portion is $\frac{1}{4}$″- or $\frac{1}{2}$″-mesh hardware cloth held to the inside of the angle framing members by strips of $\frac{1}{8}$″ x $\frac{3}{4}$″ bar stock. Make the frame first; install embossed-sheet splash guards, then hardware cloth. Fit door, attach hinges, and latch.

Note that bottom front frame member is mounted up $1\frac{1}{8}$″ above level of frame

10–11

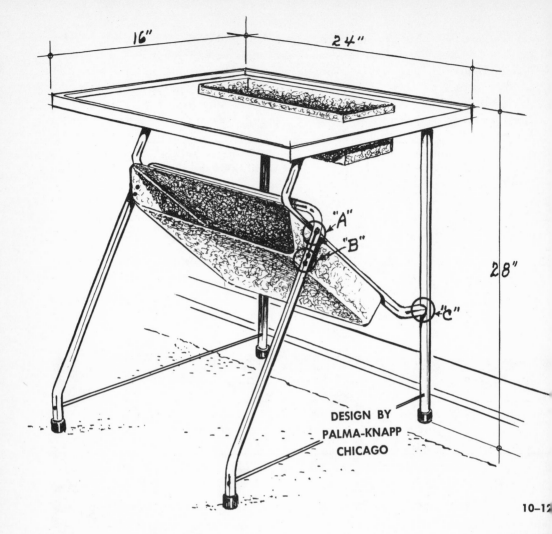

16"　　　　24"

28"

"A"
"B"
"C"

DESIGN BY
PALMA-KNAPP
CHICAGO

10-12

members at bottom of side and back panels. Notice also that the lower $1\frac{1}{8}''$ of the front face of the vertical posts at front corners is cut away to permit the tray to slide in and out. This tray is framed from 1" angle separately to over-all dimensions of $35\frac{3}{4}''$ x $11\frac{7}{8}''$, and a sheet of embossed aluminum $\frac{1}{4}''$ shorter and narrower is riveted inside this frame. An extra piece of 1" angle reinforces and stiffens the tray at the center.

STAND (*Fig. 10–11*) uses $\frac{3}{4}''$ tube cut 30" long for legs, $\frac{1}{16}''$ x 1" x 1" angle for upper frame and shelf frame. Stand is $35\frac{1}{2}''$ long, $17\frac{1}{2}''$ deep. Since stand has no top, being merely a structural support for the flight cage, attach the legs to the frame by bolting directly to tube. Each top corner reinforcement is two thick-

nesses of plain sheet 3" deep and 3" on each wing. Rivet to angle, and attach to tube legs with sheet-metal self-tapping screws or through bolts.

Shelf framing members wrap around legs and have $\frac{3}{4}''$ holes drilled through upper face at corners to accommodate the tube legs. See *Fig. 4–44* for details of this joint. Use two sheet-metal screws through angle into joint on each end and each side (four per leg) for maximum strength. Install white rubber crutch tips on feet.

Cut $\frac{3}{4}''$ plywood panel to fit shelf frame, face with embossed sheet, and rivet to frame members, completing stand.

TELEPHONE STAND WITH PLANTER (*Fig. 10–12*) employs top frame of $\frac{1}{16}''$ x 1" x 1" angle with $\frac{1}{2}''$ plywood panel set into it. A planter box 4" wide, 4" deep, 16" long

of embossed sheet is suspended in the table top by small aluminum nails driven through sides of box into edge of hole.

Make back legs 27½″ long of 1¼″ tube set into table top with blocks per instructions accompanying *Fig. 4–57*. Back legs are 4″ from each end, 2″ from back edge. Book-holder box is 18″ wide, 4″ high, 11″ deep on top side, about 9½″ on bottom side. Make from embossed sheet, and put ¼″ hem around front opening, inside, per *Fig. 3–5*. Brace to which front legs are bolted at "A" is a single piece of ¾″ tube extending from back leg to box along right-hand edge of box and up at right angles to underside of table, across underside of table, back down to another right-angle bend, down alongside the left edge of box to left back leg. Bolt to box at three points down each edge. Fasten to underside of table with straps of ⅛″ x ¾″ bar. Join at "C" per *Fig. 4–64*.

Front legs are another single piece of ¾″ tube, bent as shown and bolted to the brace at "A" and with two more bolts at "B." Now end-rivet ⅜″ rod stretchers from front to back legs 2½″ above the floor per *Fig. 4–21*. Add rubber or plastic bumpers to bottom of legs.

FLOOR LAMP (*Fig. 10–13*) features clean, simple lines that fit into almost any decor. Cut the 12″ diameter circular base from a piece of 2″ thick oak or maple. Drill a ¾″ diameter hole vertically through it 2″ in from the edge. Drive into it a 6′ length of ¾″ tube. Drill a ⅜″ diameter hole from the edge of the base to the ¾″ hole, for the electric cord. Run the lamp cord through this hole, up through the ¾″ tube, and out to a lamp fitting and socket, obtainable at your electric shop.

Attach socket and fitting to end of tube and pull extra cord back down into tube.

Bend top 16″ length of tube down to angle shown, using a 6″ radius and following instructions for tube bending accompanying *Fig. 3–27.* Polish tube with steel wool and wax to avoid finger marks. Stain and varnish wood base any color desired. Attach shade to lamp socket.

BEVERAGE SERVER (*Fig. 10–14*) requires one 6′ length of ¾″ tube and a 6′ length of ⅛″ x ¾″ x ¾″ angle. Cut tube to 36″ lengths. Bend each in center on 5″ radius so ends are 14″ apart. Attach white rubber crutch tips.

Make frame 12″ wide, 24″ long by bending and notching corners as shown in *Fig. 4–39.* Make frame ends butt together in center of back side. Cut panel from tempered Masonite or ¼″ plywood to fit inside frame. Screw, bolt, or rivet to frame. Cut 4″ x 18″ block for glasses from ¾″ plywood and use scroll saw or jig saw to make the six 2¾″ holes which are staggered as shown.

Assemble frame to leg members with bolts or self-tapping sheet-metal screws positioning the frame about 3″ underneath the bend in the tubes.

Chapter 11 . . .

PROJECTS FOR THE LIVING ROOM

SERVING WAGON (*Fig. 11–1*) has top 20″ wide, 26″ long, plus ice box. Shelf under top is also 20″ wide, 38″ long. Bottom shelf is 20″ wide, 40″ long. Make the three shelf frames first, using 1/8″ x 3/4″ x 3/4″ angle, cut and mitered at corners. Corners of top two frames are joined by riveting to vertical corner posts of 1/16″ x 1″ x 1″ angle and 8″ long, per *Fig. 4–43*. A small section of this same angle connects corners of bottom frame. Insert 1/4″ plywood panels in top two frames; use 3/4″ x 1 1/2″ slats for bottom shelf. Attach by screws up through angle into bottom of shelves. Face top-panel surface with embossed sheet cemented per instructions

to be found near the end of Chap. 4.

Use 6" rubber-tired wheels. Front and back legs extend up at 60° angle, although back legs can be at a steeper angle if desired. Legs and handle frame are also ¾" angle. Double-rivet joints, and use reinforcing plates at corners, per *Fig. 4–46*. Add ⅛" x ¾" cross braces under back legs to stiffen the structure. The handle is a piece of ¾" tube 20" long, with dowel rod inserts to permit attaching to frame with screws into tube ends, per *Fig. 4–68*.

Ice box is 8" deep, 19½" wide, 12" front to back at top, with inside surface sloping to 10" at bottom. Make as a box section (lay out per *Fig. 3–6*) from a single sheet of embossed aluminum 26½" x 36". Put ¼" hem (*Fig. 3–5*) around top edge. Overlap and rivet corners per *Fig. 4–7*. Make watertight by applying mastic into corners.

INLAID COCKTAIL TABLE (*Fig. 11–2*) features seven ¼" x 1" bars inlaid in the top and spaced 1½" apart. First build up a panel of black walnut by gluing together enough boards 1½" or 1¼" thick to produce the table top, which measures 52" x 17½" over all. A jointer makes this an easy assignment. Now sand top smooth and level.

Inlay top before working tapers. Make a straight square edge down the length of one side. Using this edge against rip fence, use bench saw to cut slots into table top to fit bars exactly. If you have a dado head available for your saw, this inlaying is easy. Adjust the head to make a 1" cut just a trifle over ¼" deep. Hold the reference edge steadily against the rip fence to get straight cuts. If you have no dado head, make regular saw cuts, setting rip fence carefully each time to get a slot just exactly 1" wide. Then use a wood chisel to remove material between saw cuts. Be sure bottom of cuts is deep enough and even.

Try fitting bar into each slot separately. If bar does not sink in slightly below

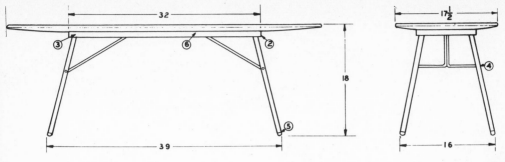

level of wood, clean out slot or cut deeper. Secure bars in slots by gluing all three sides of slot. Hold bars fully into slots with scrap wood and C-clamps. Use 1″ #8 flat-head aluminum screws at three points on each bar . . . . center and 6″ from each end. Make screws invisible by countersinking so bottom of screw slot is above surface of bar. See *Fig. 4–32* and accompanying instructions. Grind off top of screws. Sand entire top of table down smooth and level with portable belt sander.

Outline of table top tapers from 17½″ at center to 15″ at each end (see *Fig. 11–3*). So cut this outline first, using a smooth curve for the taper, not a straight line. Thickness of table top reduces sharply toward ends and sides. To work this down, turn table top over and mark out 10″ x 32″ in the center. This area will not be reduced. But tapering from this area, ends are reduced to ½″ thickness at the tips and sides to ¾″ along the edge. Use a belt sander to cut this down and to round off the finished edges smoothly.

Make a 10″ x 32″ rectangular frame (item 2, *Fig. 11–3*) from four pieces of ⅛″ x ¾″ x ¾″ angle, mitering corner joints and using splice plates as in *Fig. 4–33*. Turn table top upside down, and screw to underside of table with the flat face of angles against table. The other flat face of angles should face outward. Be sure you have made frame this way.

Cut four ¾″ tube 17″ long for the legs. Drill legs 6″ from top for the ⅜″ rod bracing; end-rivet to legs per *Fig. 4–21*. Make 90° bend in rods approximately 5½″ from end joining to legs. Make

another 90° bend in the same direction 12″ farther along bar. Allow 2″ more at this point for attaching rod to underside of table, and cut off rod. Rivet rod together in pairs as shown in *Fig. 11–2*. Secure rod to underside of table (at "6," *Fig. 11–3*) with 3″ straps of ⅛″ x ¾″ bar bent to go halfway around rod and screwed to underside of table.

Before attaching rod, secure rod to table legs and fasten legs in corner of angle framework with a bolt at "3," *Fig. 11–3*, through end of 1″ angle frame and another through side of frame. Be sure legs are positioned 16″ wide overall at floor level and 39″ apart as shown in *Fig. 11–3*.

Finish by polishing all aluminum surfaces with steel wool. Blend off all corners, and sand perfectly smooth. Apply sealer coat to table top after cutting slots and after installing the bar. Apply two heavy wipe-on coats of clear plastic finish for beautiful deep glasslike surface.

COCKTAIL TABLE WITH MAGAZINE RACK (*Fig. 11–4*) has top surface 20″ wide, 38″ long, trimmed with ¼″ x 1″ bar on edge. One piece of bar goes down the front side and half the length of each end. Other piece goes down the back side and meets the first in the center at each end. Attach bar to the ½″ thick plywood panels (12″ x 20″) with screws as in *Fig. 4–32*.

Form the center-depressed section from 21″ x 23″ embossed sheet. Make the bottom surface 14″ long, sides 4″ deep, with a 1″ flange on each end for attaching to the underside of the end panels. Paint panels black. Cut and fit a piece of double-

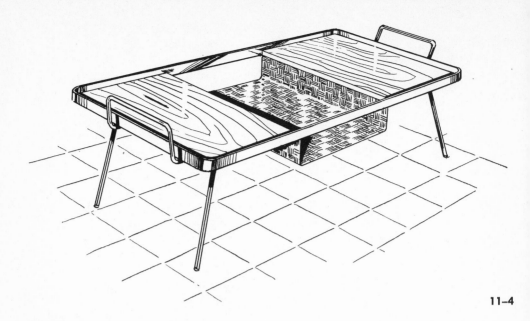

weight glass to cover entire table top (approximately 20″ x 38″). Note that outside corners of end panels and glass top must be rounded (about 1″ radius) to fit the inside bend of the bar.

Legs are ⅜″ rod, bent so that one piece forms both legs and handle at one end. Handle is 8″ long and extends 2″ above top of bar edging. Cut legs so table top is 16″ or 18″ above floor. Round off bottom of legs, or add rubber tips per Chap. 4.

DOUBLE COCKTAIL TABLE (*Fig. 11–5*) is a novel design ideal for various types of table groupings. Both table tops are ½″ plywood framed with ¼″ x 1″ bar on edge attached with invisible screws, per *Fig. 4–32* and accompanying instructions. Top table is 18″ wide at the planter end, 22″ wide at other. Lower table is 16″ wide under the intersection and 10″ wide at the free end. Make all corners with 2″ radius curves.

At the intersection of the two tables, use two 17½″ lengths of ¾″ tube for legs, set into blocks, per instructions accompanying *Fig. 4–57*. Opposite ends of both tables use ⅜″ rod supports with 3″ sections bent at right angles at top for screwing against underside of tables. Make bottom bends on 1″ radius. Planter box is embossed sheet 5″ deep sunk flush with

table top and made to fit an 8″ x 14″ opening in table.

COCKTAIL TABLE (*Fig. 11–6*) is highly modern design with exceptionally attractive appearance when finished in deep lustrous black for the wood parts and bright satin finish for the aluminum. Use cull door for top, or cut ¾″ plywood panel to 16″ x 42″ and increase thickness at edges to 1½″ with 3″ wide strips of ¾″ plywood screwed underneath all around the edge.

Begin table ends by cutting 3½″ x 10″ wood blocks which must be a full 1″ in thickness to match the ¼″ x 1″ bar stock. Cut two pieces of this bar stock 25¼″ long. Starting from the bottom (*Fig. 11–7*), make a 30° bend 1″ from end of bar. Clamp in vise between two wood blocks, and make bend by hammering with rubber mallet. Do not bend past 30°.

Now 6″ from this bend, form a 60° bend in the same direction as the first. Make the same two bends in the second leg. Next assemble these two legs to the 3½″ x 10″ wood separator, using two ⅜″ rods as big rivets. To be sure of proper assembly, examine *Fig. 4–31* carefully. Countersink bar surfaces for invisible riveting, per *Fig. 4–31* and associated instructions.

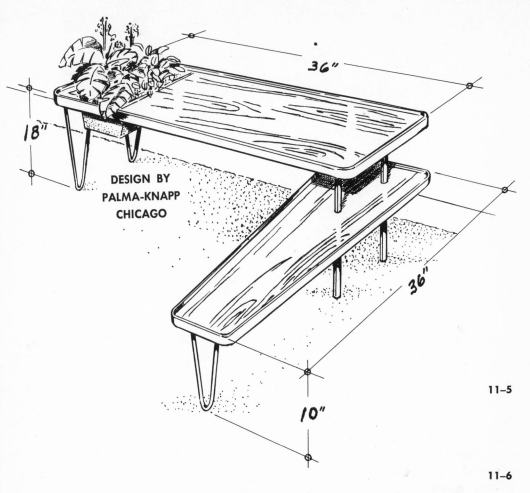

36"

18"

DESIGN BY
PALMA-KNAPP
CHICAGO

36"

10"

11–5

11–6

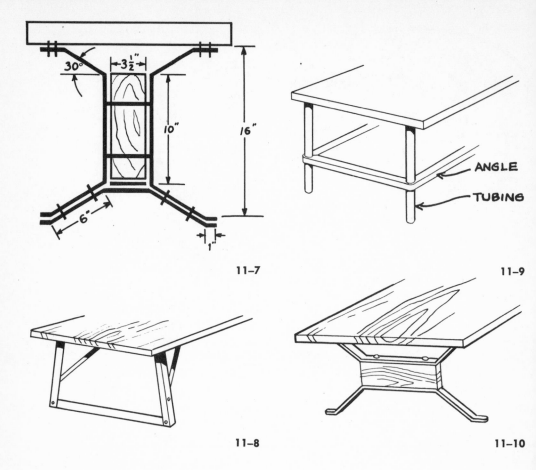

11-7

11-9

11-8

11-10

Continue bending the two legs by clamping in a vise and making 60° bends at top of separator block as shown in *Fig. 11-7*. A 30° bend 6″ from this last bend completes the legs. Drill two holes in top end of each leg for screws into underside of table top.

Fit a 3½″ piece of 1″ bar just below the separator block (*Fig. 11-7*). Cut a piece of 1″ bar about 18″ long, and bend to fit snugly under the two legs as shown. Rivet this piece to both legs on the sloping side as indicated. Countersink for "invisible" riveting.

Attach each pair of legs to the table, and install a brace of 1″ bar stock to center of each separator block (*Fig. 11-6*). Satin-finish all the aluminum with fine sandpaper, and apply wax or clear lacquer.

COCKTAIL TABLE . . . . ANGLE LEGS (*Fig. 11-8*) employs 1/16″ x 1″ x 1″ angle for

legs and bottom brace with the corner bends made as in *Fig. 4-41* and locked by riveting the overlapped sections. Top end of legs is cut, bent, and screwed to underside of table top, per *Fig. 4-47*. Braces are 3/4″ bar riveted to leg and bent over at upper end to permit screwing to table.

Since cocktail tables vary in size from 3′ to 4′ or more in length, 16″ to 24″ in width, and 16″ to 18″ in height, proportion the legs to suit your own ideas. Inset table edge with 1/4″ bar (*Fig. 4-32*) or angle (*Fig. 4-50*).

COCKTAIL TABLE . . . . TUBE LEGS (*Fig. 11-9*) has 3/4″ tube legs set into table top with stretchers of 1/16″ x 1″ x 1″ angle. Tube-to-angle joint is made per *Fig. 4-44*. This table design has the added possibility of reversing the position of the angle frame to form a retainer for a piece of glass which then provides a shelf under the table without added structural ele-

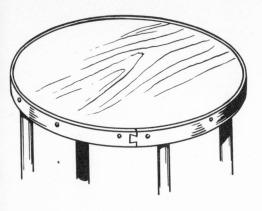

11–11

ments. Inset table edge with ¼″ bar (*Fig. 4–32*) or 1″ angle (*Fig. 4–50*).

COCKTAIL TABLE . . . . BAR LEGS (*Fig. 11–10*) offers a novel design that is easy to make following the suggestions of *Fig. 4–31*. The 1″ x 3″ wood piece is secured between the bars by two pieces of ⅜″ rod which act as huge rivets. Rod ends may be upset or countersunk flush with bar if you wish. To stiffen this design,

rivet another length of bar across the bottom as a stretcher. Finish by installing ¼″ bar as table edge (*Fig. 4–32*) or by insetting 1″ angle (*Fig. 4–50*).

ROUND TABLES: The design shown in *Fig. 11–11* is adaptable to a wide variety of sizes. After cutting out a top of ¾″ plywood, smooth the edge with a rasp and apply ¼″ x 1″ bar by attaching one end (see *Fig. 4–32*) and simply wrapping the bar around the table. Use a rubber or wood mallet to get the desired curvature at bar ends. Join the two bar ends with the dovetail joint (*Fig. 4–28*) or the lap-type joint (*Fig. 4–26 or 27*).

The legs will be self-supporting if table top is of two thicknesses of ¾″ plywood, or use additional plywood blocks at points where legs attach so at least a 1¼″ deep hole can be provided for ¾″ tube legs.

For large-sized tables, use 1″ or 1¼″ tube for legs with correspondingly thicker blocks to provide hole depth required. See instructions for attaching legs accompanying *Fig. 4–57*.

11–12

Low Stool: The design shown in *Fig. 11–11* provides sufficient strength for low stools for children's use in play or watching TV. For added strength, use a ⅛″ x ¾″ bar as a stretcher around all four legs.

Magazine Rack (*Fig. 11–12*) requires two pieces of union-jack perforated sheet 12″ x 15½″ for the sides, one 14″ x 16″ embossed sheet for the center divider, another 7″ x 16″ embossed sheet for the bottom, two 8″ x 12″ plain sheets for ends, four 14″ lengths of ¾″ tube for the legs, and a 22″ length of ¼″ x 1″ bar stock for the handle.

Make top frame first, using 1⁄16″ x 1″ x 1″ angle to inside dimensions of 7½″ x 15″. Cut sides 17″ long, ends 9½″ long, and saw 45° *outside* miters at corners. Join at corners with splice plate also cut from 1″ angle and riveted as per *Fig. 4–35*.

11–13

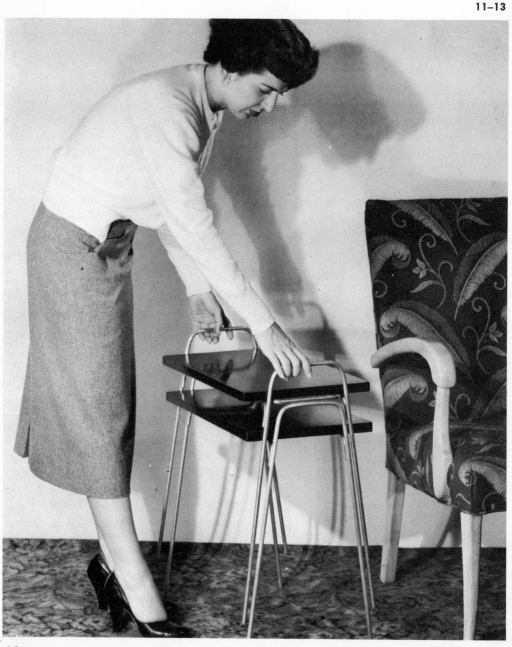

Flange ends of perforated side sheets to fit this frame, and turn a $\frac{1}{4}''$ flange underneath at the bottom edge. Rivet frame to top of side sheets. Cut end sheets on a center line so they taper from 8" at the top to 7" at the bottom. Turn up a 90° flange $\frac{1}{4}''$ wide on each sloping side and underneath at the bottom edge. Now rivet frame to top edge of end sheets, being sure flanges overlap the side sheets.

Assemble legs to the structure, using sheet-metal self-tapping screws to hold the assembly as in *Fig. 4–80,* a cross section of the left front leg.

Hem edges of bottom sheet (*Fig. 3–5*) so it covers exactly $6\frac{1}{2}''$ x 15", insert it in the structure so it lies on bottom flanges of side and end sheets, and rivet to these flanges. Next flange center divider sheet all around to measure exactly $11\frac{7}{8}''$ x 15". Hem top edge. Rivet end and bottom flanges of divider to end and bottom sheets.

Drill an opening in the center of top end frames for the handle. Enlarge opening with a small saw and file to exactly $\frac{1}{4}''$ x 1" to take handle. Bend handle to fit, insert in holes, and rivet to end sheets. Polish legs, top frame, and end sheets with steel wool, and apply wax or clear lacquer.

NESTING TABLES (*Fig. 11–13*) are useful as a telephone stand, end table, or eating table for the children watching TV. Cut out the 12" x 18" table top from $\frac{3}{4}''$ plywood, oak, maple, or just plain pine, and finish it preferably in a dark color to contrast to the bright aluminum $\frac{3}{8}''$ bar used as legs and brackets. Notice that Part "A" in *Fig. 11–14* allows tables to be nested (*Fig. 11–13*) without damage to table tops.

Cut two A members $12\frac{5}{8}''$ long; two B's 22" long; two C's 50" long. Cut out form block for C's, and bend C's around it. Put 90° bends into B's approximately 2" in from each end so space between outer surfaces is 18", per *Fig. 11–14.* Now rivet B's to C's, and attach table top with screws up through B's.

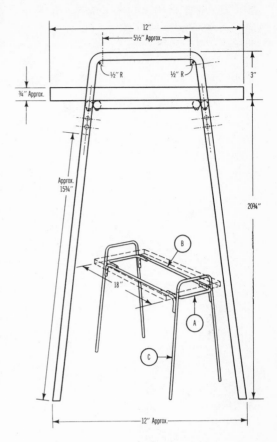

11–14

Put two 90° bends in A's about $2\frac{1}{2}''$ in from each end. After bending, A's should just fit between C's as shown. Position A's so they extend out from the table top the same distance as C's, and attach with screws up into the table top.

UNIQUE ROOM DIVIDER (*Fig. 11–15*) is exceptionally attractive, although it has more elements and thus takes longer to build than the thin model shown in *Fig. 11–18.* Referring to item numbers in *Fig. 11–16,* cut the following materials to sizes specified:

Item 1, tempered Masonite ($\frac{1}{8}''$ thick) $2\frac{3}{4}''$ x $47\frac{7}{8}''$; item 2, $\frac{3}{4}''$ plywood $13\frac{1}{8}''$ x $47\frac{7}{8}''$; item 3, wood 2" x 4" x $13\frac{1}{8}''$, two pieces; item 4, two 1" aluminum tubes $61\frac{1}{2}''$; item 5, two 1" tubes 62"; item 6, $\frac{3}{4}''$ plywood $13\frac{3}{4}''$ x $47\frac{7}{8}''$; item 7, two $\frac{3}{4}''$ aluminum angles $13\frac{3}{8}''$; item 8, $\frac{1}{4}$-20 x $1\frac{1}{4}''$ round-head machine screws, 23 re-

quired; item 9, ¾″ plywood 14⅞″ x 47⅞″; item 10, two ¾″ angles 14½″; item 11, tempered Masonite 15″ x 47⅞″; item 12, ¾″ plywood 16″ x 47⅝″; item 13, two ¾″ angles 49⅝″; item 14, two pieces Masonite 15⅞″ x 17⅜″; item 15, two wood ¾″ x ¾″ x 14¼″; item 16, 23 hex nuts ¼-20; item 17, ¾″ plywood 17⅜″ x 47⅝″; item 18, two pieces perforated Masonite 14½″ x 24½″; item 19, 21 round-head wood screws #5 x ⅝″; item 20, 18 round-head wood screws #6 x ¾″; item 21, six finishing nails 8 penny.

Prepare top-shelf ends (item 3) by drilling a 1″ diameter hole 1″ from rear end in both pieces; then drill a 1″ hole 10¾″ from center of this hole for front leg. Use a 5° wedge block as in *Fig. 4–57* to put this hole in line with the front legs . . . . all holes are 1½″ deep. Cut a ⅛″ wide vertical slot ⅜″ from back end and ¼″ deep for top-shelf back (item 1). Because there is a right and a left end piece, be sure to cut grooves on *inside*

faces. Next cut a ¾″ groove ¾″ wide and ½″ from bottom of piece for top shelf (item 2). Now taper from 3½″ height at back to 2½″ high at front by cutting off top edge.

Prepare item 2 by cutting a ⅛″ wide groove ¼″ deep full length. Now round off front upper corner on upper side ⅜″ in from back edge to receive item 1. Bevel front edge of this and all other shelves to a 5° angle to match slope of front legs.

Rabbet back edge of items 12 and 17, ⅛″ wide, ⅛″ deep to receive cabinet back, item 11.

Notch ends of items 6, 9, 12, and 17 to clear nuts. For "A" in *Fig. 11–16*, see detail in *Fig. 4–74*. Bend cabinet angle frames, item 13, per *Fig. 4–39*. Make first bend exactly 17⁷⁄₁₆″ from end for the bottom corner and exactly 15½″ farther for the top corner bend. This will make the bottom piece 17⅝″ over all; front section, 15⅞″; top section, 16¼″.

Start assembly operations by turning

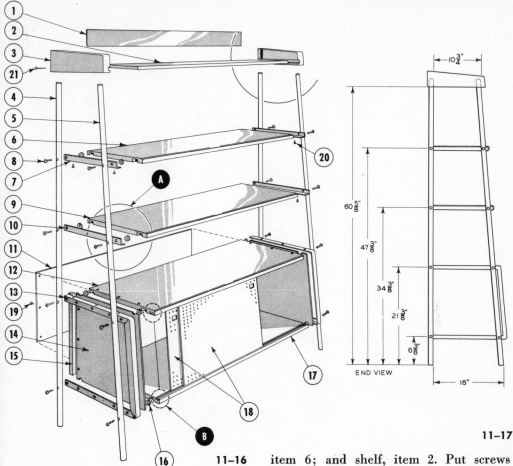

END VIEW

11–17

11–16

all four legs into upper-shelf ends, item 3. Lay out left end structure on the floor per *Fig. 11–17*, and drill holes through back leg at points indicated. Attach angle frame, item 13, to back leg, clamping together the members to be joined using C-clamps, then drilling and bolting. Indent holes for bolts per *Fig. 4–73*. Next position front leg, clamp, drill, and bolt. Use the same sequence in attaching shelf supports, items 7 and 10, being careful to square them up with the back leg before drilling and bolting to the front leg. Now lay out the other end of structure on the floor and assemble, remembering this is right-hand, the first one left-hand.

Now build up structure by attaching cabinet sides, item 14; the cabinet cleats, item 15; the cabinet bottom, item 17; cabinet top, item 12; shelf, item 9; shelf,

item 6; and shelf, item 2. Put screws through item 13 up into bottom of item 17 first; then position all other members; now put screws up through item 7 into bottom of item 6. If the length of shelf members is not exactly right, make corrections at this point. Then put screws into shelves, items 9 and 12; attach cabinet back, item 13; and slip top shelf back into place.

Cut finger holes into the perforated Masonite sliding doors, paint them white, and assemble to cabinet. For brilliant aluminum finish, scrub with steel wool, sand with fine sandpaper, and apply wax or clear lacquer. Wood parts should be black enameled or lacquered after sealing.

If necessary, adjust leg lengths to make structure set square.

THIN WALL DIVIDER (*Fig. 11–18*) is ideal where not too much space is available. Use ¾″ tube for legs. The back leg is

60″ long, front slightly longer. Use ⅛″ x ¾″ x ¾″ angle for framework.

Start by making box frame for upper cupboard 54″ long, 14″ high, 6″ deep. Or you can omit the longitudinal aluminum members and use the ¾″ plywood top and bottom only. In either case, cut and attach end panels of ¾ plywood to fit end frames.

Construct lower cabinet 36″ long, 18″ high, 9″ deep, using ¾″ angle framing. Here again, only the left-hand end frame is absolutely necessary, the rest of the box section being self-supporting if made from

¾″ plywood. Note that cabinet bottom extends the full width of divider, 54″ between leg members.

The full-length (54″) shelf above lower cabinet is also 9″ deep.

Slot upper and lower cabinet shelves to take sliding doors, per *Fig. 4–82*. Cut perforated Masonite panels to fit. Cut back panels for both upper and lower cabinets, and assemble to cabinets. With both cabinets completed and finished (satin black is recommended), place them face down on the floor.

Clamp back leg to lower cabinet so it

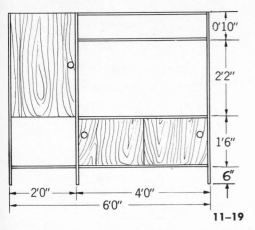

0'10"

2'2"

1'6"

6"

2'0" · 4'0"

6'0"

11–19

will be 11" from floor (when upright). Drill lower bolt hole through tube and angle frame, indent per *Fig. 4–73*, and insert wood screw into cabinet. Drill, indent, and screw leg to upper portion of cabinet. Now clamp center shelf and its angle support to the back leg so bottom of shelf is 3" above top of lower cabinet. Then drill back leg and angle, indent, and insert wood screw at this point.

Now position top of upper cabinet even with upper end of leg, clamp, drill, indent, and insert wood screws in both top and bottom of this cabinet. Next attach the other back leg to opposite points on cabinets and shelves.

To position front leg, turn cabinets over with back to floor, clamp top of tube to the mid-point of top end-frame member of the top cabinet (4" from back). Drill through tube and angle, indent, and insert wood screw into cabinet. Now position bottom end of front leg so the inside distance between the front and back legs at the floor level is exactly 7½". Clamp in this position, drill through tube and angle at bottom of lower cabinet, indent, and insert wood screw into cabinet. The front leg is now positioned so it can be attached to the lower member of the upper cabinet, to the shelf, and to the upper frame member of the lower cabinet. Be sure to position center shelf so it is square with back leg before attaching to front leg.

Now install the sliding doors, and attach the two vertical frame strips (⅛" x

¾" bar) 18" from each end in the top cabinet. The two silver drawers below the top cabinet measure 17¾" wide over all, 6" deep, 2" high. Make from ½" plywood, and slot upper outside surfaces ⅜" from top and ¼" deep to fit the drawer slides, made from U-shaped strips of plain aluminum sheet screwed to the bottom of upper cabinet. See *Fig. 4–83* for details.

STORAGE DIVIDER (*Fig. 11–19*) combines a storage cabinet, considerable shelf area, and a room divider. While other dimensions can easily be adopted, the unit shown measures 6' wide, 5' high, and 20" deep. Storage cabinet at left is 3' high, 2' wide. Lower cabinet is 18" high, 4' wide. Notice that the bottom of lower cabinet extends the full width of the unit and that the top section of upper cabinet also extends the full width of unit. The shelf near the top, of course, is only 4' wide.

The only aluminum used in this design are the six 5' lengths of ⅛" x ¾" x ¾" angle used for the legs. To construct this unit, make and assemble the two cabinets. Remember that top of the upper cabinet, top and bottom of lower cabinet extend the full width of the unit (6'). Then attach the aluminum legs with wood screws. Either install sliding doors (per *Fig. 4–82*), or attach hinges for doors which may be either plywood or Masonite.

MODIFIED STORAGE DIVIDER (*Fig. 11–20*) is made to exactly the same dimensions as the unit of *Fig. 11–19*. It has a more distinctive touch, however, due to its novel combination of wood and glass. This unit utilizes a ⅛" x ¾" x ¾" angle frame for the shelf just under the top and for the lower left-hand shelf as well. Then a piece of double-weight window glass is cut to fit and set in place after covering edges with Scotch tape to prevent glass-to-metal contact.

Corners of these angle frames adjoining the wood are bent, per *Fig. 4–39*. Corners fitting into legs are cut to length, mitered, and riveted inside legs. Use wood screws to attach frame to wood panels.

11–20

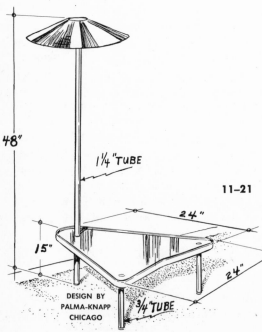

11–21

48″

1¼″ TUBE

24″

15″

24″

¾″ TUBE

DESIGN BY
PALMA-KNAPP
CHICAGO

FLOOR LAMP—TABLE COMBINATION (*Fig. 11–21*) will add a modern touch to any setting when finished in black lacquer and satin aluminum. Yet it's so simple to make. Cut a ½″ plywood panel into a triangle measuring 24″ on each side. At the peak of this triangle, mark off a 4″ radius instead of the sharp corner, and drill a 1¼″ hole at center of this radius.

On the other two corners, mark off 2″ radii instead of the sharp pointed corner and drill ¾″ holes on centers so located. Note from *Fig. 11–21* that the front edge of table is not a straight line but a V. Measure to the center of this side of the table, and put a mark out 2″ toward the lamp post. From this point, mark a straight line back to the two front corners, and cut along this line.

Now bend a 6′ length of ¼″ x 1″ bar on edge to fit around the table, making the two ends come together at the center of the V. Anchor one end of bar into the V with wood screws. See *Fig. 4–32* and accompanying instructions. Then wrap bar around table edge with table clamped securely to workbench, using a rubber mallet to aid forming. Anchor with another screw as each side is completed. Cut free end to fit into the V, and attach with two more "invisible" screws.

Add three small braces (of $\frac{1}{8}''$ x $\frac{3}{4}''$ bar) under table around $1\frac{1}{4}''$ tube to reinforce its connection to table. Front legs have added $\frac{1}{2}''$ plywood block under table for additional grip on tube. Close top and bottom of front legs with snap-in closures, as well as bottom of other leg. The lamp shade is a cone of plain sheet, 18″ diameter, 3″ deep, with a 3″ hole in the top. The lamp socket comes with small tube, which you fit into the top of lamp support by inserting a block in top of $1\frac{1}{4}''$ tube and drilling to fit. Support shade with a spring clip from any old lamp shade available.

Chapter 12 . . .

PROJECTS FOR THE PORCH, TERRACE, LAWN

LAWN CANE TRAY (*Fig. 12–1*) is handy outside anywhere as it is held in position by pushing the sharpened point into the ground. The $\frac{3}{8}''$ rod is in two sections joined end to end at the tray with a stud bolt as detailed in *Fig. 4–14*. A washer on each side of the tray spreads the stresses and strengthens the sheet-to-rod joint. Cut the washers out of a piece of 1″ x 1″ x $\frac{1}{16}''$ angle, and drill to fit the stud.

The bottom section of the rod is 36″ long; the top piece is 18″ with the handle curved on a 4″ radius. The tray is 12″ in diameter, made of two thicknesses of aluminum sheet joined by two or three rivets in each scallop for maximum strength and stiffness.

LAWN SPRINKLER (*Fig. 12–2*) employs a 6′ or 8′ length of $\frac{3}{4}''$ tube fitted with a hose coupler at one end as shown in *Fig. 4–81*. The other end is flattened and riveted to a 14″ length of $\frac{1}{4}''$ x 1″ bar, which is turned down at each end to carry small wheels of plywood. Drill two rows of $\frac{1}{32}''$ holes down the length of the tube, spaced about 2″ apart or closer if desired.

ALL-ALUMINUM CARD TABLE (*Fig. 12–3*) uses a frame 36″ x 36″ of $\frac{1}{16}''$ x 1″ x 1″ angle with corners carefully mitered and

12–1

DOUBLE SHEET

DRILL $\frac{1}{4}''$ HOLE FOR STUD BOLT

POINTED $\frac{3}{8}$ ROD

12–2

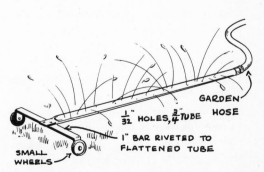

GARDEN HOSE

$\frac{1}{32}''$ HOLES, $\frac{3}{4}''$ TUBE

1″ BAR RIVETED TO FLATTENED TUBE

SMALL WHEELS

joined by bolting the special Stanley hinge bracket (*Fig. 12–4*) (available in most hardware stores) inside at each corner. Center-punch and drill ¼″ holes for the ¼″ x 1″ bolts. Trim a full sheet of embossed aluminum 36″ x 36″ to fit under the Stanley brackets, and rivet to the underside of angle frame, spacing rivets 2″ apart around the entire frame and ½″ in from the edge. Put ¾″ x 2″ redwood strips crosswise underneath the metal sheet to stiffen and prevent sagging. Where strips cross each other, make a saw cut and chisel out half of each member to make a lap joint, like *Fig. 4–29*. Put wood screws through edge of frame angles into ends of braces to secure in place.

Cut four legs 27″ long from 1″ tube. Turn table frame upside down. Lay the four legs along inside of frame. Clamp legs under the Stanley brackets, allowing

¼″ clearance between end of leg and frame. Use a ⅜″ wood spacer block between leg and inside of angle frame to position legs correctly under the Stanley bracket. Drill four ⅛″ holes, and screw four #8 x ¾″ self-tapping screws through bracket arm into each tube leg.

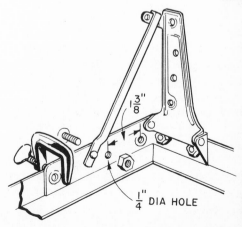

¾″

¼″ DIA HOLE

94

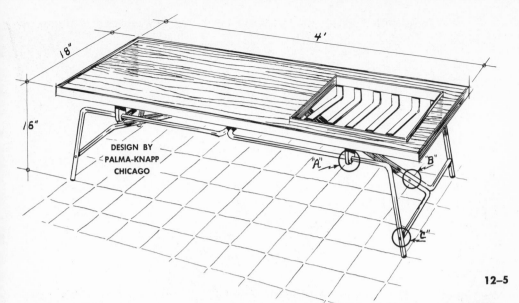

18"

16"

4'

DESIGN BY
PALMA-KNAPP
CHICAGO

"A" "B" "C"

12–5

Note that there is a pin alongside the bracket to guide the folding arm or latch. Pull leg up, and mark location for pin. Drill ⅛" hole through the arm hole into the leg. Drive the pin furnished with the Stanley bracket into the hole in the leg up to the shoulder. Leg will now latch in fully open position, yet can be folded down flat into table frame.

PLANTER COFFEE TABLE (*Fig. 12–5*) combines a coffee or cocktail table with a recessed section for a planter . . . . or an aquarium for fish. Filled with brightly colored fish, marine plants, etc., this makes a highly novel combination. Table top is ¾" plywood, edged all around with ¹⁄₁₆" x 1" x 1" angle bent around corners (per *Fig. 4–37*) and screwed to underside of table.

Make the four legs from ¾" tube and bend as shown. See *Fig. 3–27* for tube bending. The support at "A" is an angle formed from ¼" x 1" bar with top section screwed to underside of table and vertical portion drilled to take the ¾" tube as shown. Lock tube in position by drilling a small hole in back edge of bar, and insert pin into tube.

Braces are ⅜" rod, riveted together at "B" and end-riveted to tube legs at "C" per *Fig. 4–21*. Aquarium supports are ¼" bar screwed to underside of table.

AQUARIUM: Make full frame from ⅛" x ¾" x ¾" angle to size desired per *Fig. 4–42*, but put vertical corner posts outside the top and bottom frames, not inside as shown in detail in *Fig. 4–43*. Miter frame corners, and rivet all connections securely. Bottom, sides, and ends are panels of ¼" plate glass. Cut bottom ⅛" smaller than inside measurements of bottom frame. Place a good fillet of Alumastic (aluminum mastic compound) inside corners of bottom frame. Then set glass into this mastic. Cut side panels ⅛" smaller than remaining space inside frame, put mastic into corners of frame members, and set glass into mastic. Now cut end panels also ⅛" smaller than space remaining, place mastic, and insert panels. Place mastic inside ends and sides all around bottom. Fill aquarium with water. Allow to set several days. If water seeps through joints, add a small amount of mastic inside the glass at joints after thoroughly drying the entire aquarium.

INDIRECT TABLE LAMP (*Fig. 12–6*) has a 5" diameter round wood base 1¼" thick which contains the lamp socket. Three ⅜" rods 3" long are equispaced around the outside by drilling ⅜" holes 1" deep into base as shown. The three legs of ⅜" rod are end-riveted to these rods at "A" per *Fig. 4–20*, at a point 4" above the

95

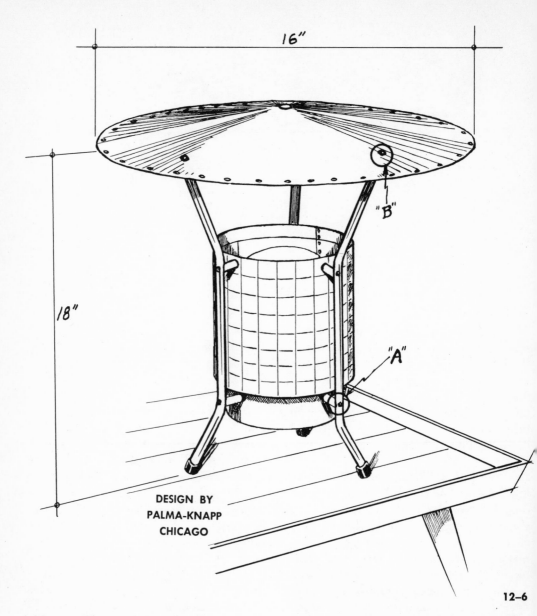

16"

18"

"B"

"A"

DESIGN BY
PALMA-KNAPP
CHICAGO

12–6

table top. Three other stud rods are end-riveted to the legs 8" above "A" in the same manner. Opposite ends of these studs are end-riveted per *Fig. 4–19* to the 7" diameter, 10" high tube of plain sheet. Scratch a rectangular pattern of 1" squares on outer face of this tube section as shown.

The lamp shade is a 16" diameter, 2" deep cone of plain sheet, end-riveted to the ends of the three legs at "B" per *Fig. 4–19*. Put rubber tips on legs, and run lamp cord out through bottom or side, as desired.

LARGE TABLE LAMP (*Fig. 12–7*) will cast a dull glow over a large floor area without shining in your face. First make the wood base section by cutting out two 4" diameter circles in ¾" plywood. Screw together. Drill three equispaced ¾" diameter holes around edge to take the legs of ¾" tube. Cut legs 13" long. Make a bend 8" from the bottom on as short a radius as you can handle. See *Fig. 3–27* and accompanying instructions for tube bending.

Insert tube in base block, and lock with screws or nails driven up from bot-

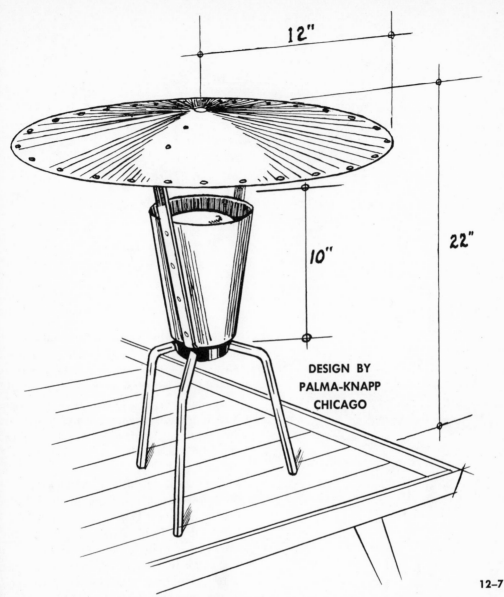

12"

22"

10"

DESIGN BY
PALMA-KNAPP
CHICAGO

12–7

tom of block into tube. File bottom of tube off flat with table top, and insert spring closure caps or a rounded wood dowel.

Screw lamp socket to top of wood base. Make cone for lamp 10″ high, 6″ diameter at bottom, 8″ diameter at top, and rivet the two top shade supports to cone. These supports are ⅛″ x ¾″ bar 18″ long. Bend bottom 2″ to go under cone, and screw to top of wood base. Bend top 2″ of support inward to fit under top shade.

Top shade is a 24″ diameter circle of plain sheet with a 1″ hole in the center and with a 1″ pie section cut out. The remaining edges are overlapped and riveted to form a cone 2″ deep. Drill a row of ¼″ diameter holes ½″ from edge, 2″ apart. Rivet to shade supports.

Picnic Table, Benches (*Fig. 12–8*) use ⅛″ x ¾″ x ¾″ angle for frame with ⅜″ rod for bracing. Table and bench surfaces are redwood 2 x 4's or ¾″ plywood. Seal all wood surfaces before assembly, and stain or leave natural. Finish with spar varnish.

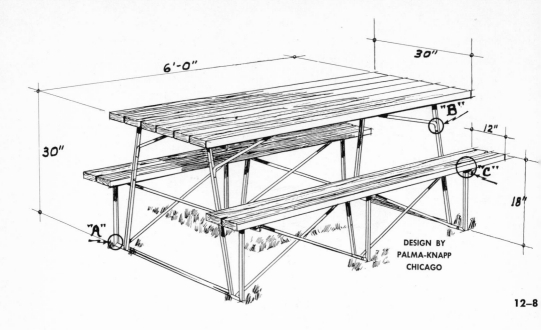

DESIGN BY
PALMA-KNAPP
CHICAGO

6'-0"   30"

30"   12"

"B"   "C"

18"

"A"

12–8

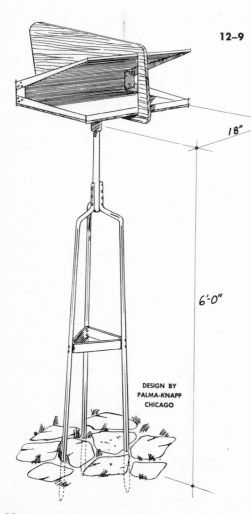

12–9

18"

6'-0"

DESIGN BY
PALMA-KNAPP
CHICAGO

Rivet in splice plates at "A" and similar points where the angle stock is bent to form corners. Flatten out, drill, and rivet ends of cross braces to the angle at "B" and similar spots. Screw through angle into underside of wood for attaching seats and table top to frame. Wood members extend 6" past frame on ends.

BIRD FEEDER (*Fig. 12–9*) employs $\frac{3}{8}$" rod for lower tripod members and $1\frac{1}{4}$" tube for top member. Tripod spacer is $\frac{1}{4}$" x 1" bar bent to form a triangle 12" on the side. Halve and overlap ends and pin, per *Fig. 4–26*. Insert a wood dowel in bottom of tube, and attach rods to tube with wood screws into this dowel.

Upper section of feeder has a $\frac{1}{4}$" plywood base 12" x 18", covered with plain sheet aluminum. Pan and lid are bent from a single piece 20" x 27". Turn up a 1" flange around bottom section, and turn down a $\frac{1}{2}$" flange on top section. Taper end flanges as shown, and rivet to back flange to support pan lid. The "weather-vane" type center support is a $\frac{1}{2}$" plywood panel with a hole cut to fit the open pan section as shown. Slot upper end of tube, and bend out sections to form flanges for attaching to underside of tray and vane, per *Fig. 4–77*.

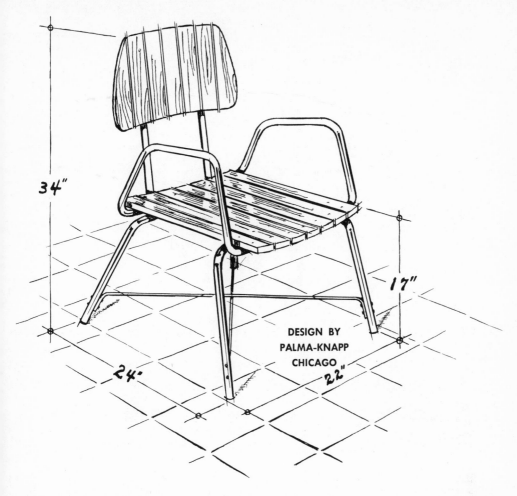

34"

17"

24"

22"

DESIGN BY
PALMA-KNAPP
CHICAGO

ARMCHAIR (*Fig. 12–10*) uses four pieces of ¾″ tube. One piece forms the front legs and a crossbar underneath the seat at the front. A second piece forms the back legs and a crossbar underneath the seat at the back. A third starts underneath the seat at the front, extends out and up to form an armrest, down and under the seat again, and back up to carry half the back rest. The fourth forms a similar member on the opposite side. The seat is made of 1″ x 3″ redwood boards 18″ long; the back rest, 10″ lengths of the same material.

None of these bends are critical. See *Fig. 3–27* and accompanying instructions on tube bending. Bolt the tubes to the seat members, countersinking boltheads on top of wood. Use ⅜″ rod for cross bracing, bolted to legs or end-riveted as in *Fig. 4–21.*

LAWN CHAIR (*Fig. 12–11*) is a novel design. It is easy to make, as the structure is very simple. Make the seat and back assembly first. Side frames are panels of 1″ maple cut to shape indicated and joined with through bolts and screws. Seat frames extend 16″ forward, so distance between front stretcher and lower back stretcher (1″ tube) is 16″ center to center. All three tubes used as stretchers are held into notches in the wood frame with screws through the tube just inside the open end. The main structural member joining side frames is "B," cut 8″ wide, 19″ long from 1″ maple or oak, and inset into side frames as shown. Attach

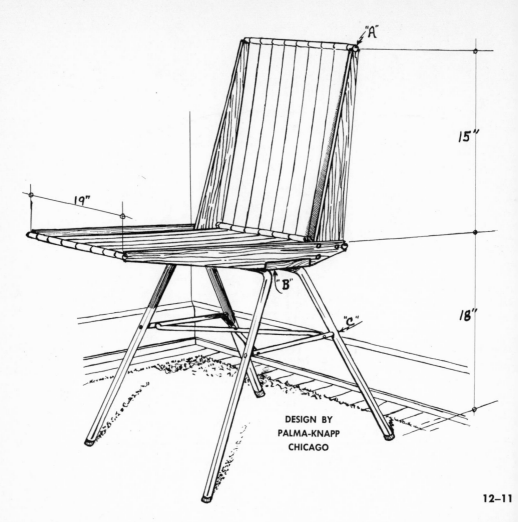

15"

19"

18"

"A"

"B"

"C"

DESIGN BY
PALMA-KNAPP
CHICAGO

12–11

with four 3″ screws into each side frame.

Form legs from two pieces of ¾″ tube. One piece makes front legs and upper crossbar; the second makes back legs and upper crossbar. Cross braces 10″ above floor are ⅜″ rod, end-riveted into tube at "C" per *Fig. 4–21* and rod to rod per *Fig. 4–20*. Attach each tube crossbar to seat member "B" with four ¼″ through bolts, countersinking heads on upper side.

Seat and back surfaces are plastic or canvas webbing. Cover top side of "B" with foam rubber for main support under web.

COCKTAIL TABLE (*Fig. 12–12*) features two large shelves for magazines and a two-level design that adds an air of distinction. This large table should be used only in a good-sized room. End panels are

20″ square, edged with 1⁄16″ x 1″ x 1″ angle that is bent down 4″ at a 60° angle both along front and back edges to the center 18″-long panel. A 6′ angle will frame one end panel and extend down to the center panel. So three lengths will be required. All panels are ¾″ plywood finished in black lacquer or Nov-A-Ply with clear lacquer. Be sure to use splice plates to reinforce corners at "A," made per *Fig. 4–37*, and at "D."

Cut the four legs from 1″ tube 16″ long, and set top ends into ¾″ plywood blocks and into underside of end panels. See *Fig. 4–57* and instructions for inserting legs. Slant legs out 10°. Brace legs with ⅜″ rod extending full length of table and end-riveted at "C" per *Fig. 4–21* and screwed against underside of center panel. Cross-bars set 2″ apart to form magazine rack

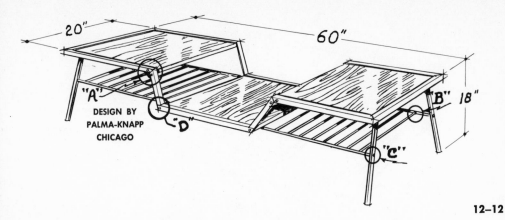

under each end are also ⅜″ rod end-riveted to long rods at "B" per *Fig. 4–20*.

BOOK MAGAZINE RACK (*Fig. 12–13*) is an ideal unit for a porch or any outdoor area, as it is all-aluminum. Panel is 16½″ wide, 24″ long, plus 4″ turnup at front. Bend side frames from ¾″ tube as shown, and pin tube edgewise into ¼″ x 1″ bar which frames the embossed sheet panel, using an aluminum nail at "B" and other contact points. Two reinforcing cross-bars of ⅜″ rod, 18¼″ long, form a book-rest at back by end-riveting into tube frames at "A" per *Fig. 4–21*. Top bar is 4″ above lower, which is 1½″ above panel. See *Fig. 3–27* and accompanying instructions for tube bending.

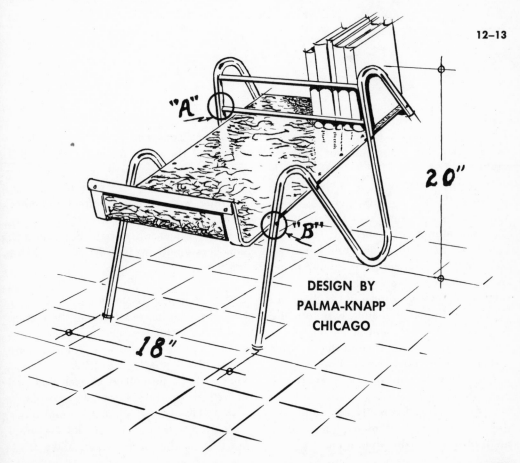

12–13

DESIGN BY
PALMA-KNAPP
CHICAGO

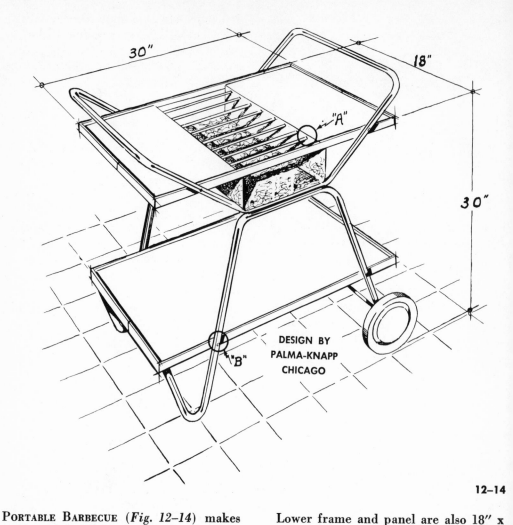

30"

18"

"A"

30"

"B"

DESIGN BY
PALMA-KNAPP
CHICAGO

12–14

PORTABLE BARBECUE (*Fig. 12–14*) makes an excellent unit for outdoor cooking. Make top frame of $\frac{1}{16}''$ x 1" x 1" angle with corners notched, bent, and reinforced with splice plates, per *Fig. 4–37*. Cut two $\frac{1}{2}''$ plywood end panels 10" x 18", and mount in frame. Cut embossed aluminum panel 18" x 36", and bend two 10" panels at each end. A third 10" panel in the center is depressed 3" below the other two panels as shown in the diagram. These are simple 90° bends, easy to make per *Fig. 3–6*. Place bent sheet on top of wood end panels, and cement in place per instructions at end of Chap. 4.

The grill is $\frac{3}{8}''$ rod spaced 2" apart and end-riveted to the sheet per *Fig. 4–19*. Do not place charcoal directly on aluminum sheet but on a piece of expanded steel mesh placed over the aluminum.

Lower frame and panel are also 18" x 30". Seal the wood panels before installing. Cement embossed sheet to upper panel surfaces. Use $\frac{3}{4}''$ tube for the end-framing with through bolts for connections to angle frames at "B." See *Fig. 4–84* for wheel-axle details. See *Fig. 3–27* and accompanying instructions for bending tube.

OUTDOOR WALL LAMP (*Fig. 12–15*) attached to the house adjoining the terrace makes an attractive lighting scheme possible . . . . especially with colored lamp bulbs. Bracket is $\frac{1}{4}''$ x 1" bar cut 14" long with 1" turned up at each end and drilled for $\frac{3}{4}''$ tube extending up to lamp socket. This is a 4" diameter wood block with a cone top as shown and hollowed out to take the lamp socket. Make lamp

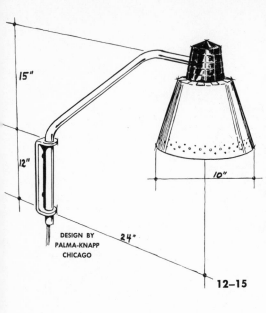

DESIGN BY
PALMA-KNAPP
CHICAGO

15"

12"

10"

24"

12-15

shade of plain aluminum sheet formed to a cone 10″ diameter at bottom and 6″ at top, 7″ deep. Form cone 10″ deep first, then slot upper 3″ and fold tips in to make flange, in turn screwed to bottom face of the wood block.

Drill or punch a series of small holes around edge of shade to let out light sidewise. To make the supporting arm, see *Fig. 3–27* and accompanying instructions on tube bending.

FLOWER STAND (*Fig. 12–16*), although presenting a highly novel and modern appearance, is simple to construct. Top frame is $\frac{1}{8}$″ x $\frac{3}{4}$″ bar 62″ long, bent at all four corners with the ends overlapped in back per *Fig. 4–26*. Lower frame is $\frac{1}{16}$″ x 1″ x 1″ angle cut and formed to the

12–16

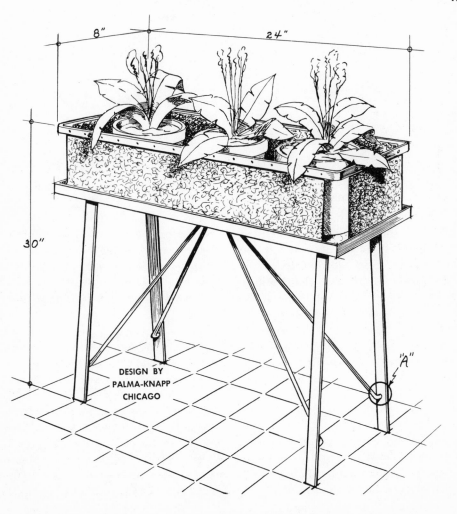

8"

24"

30"

"A"

DESIGN BY
PALMA-KNAPP
CHICAGO

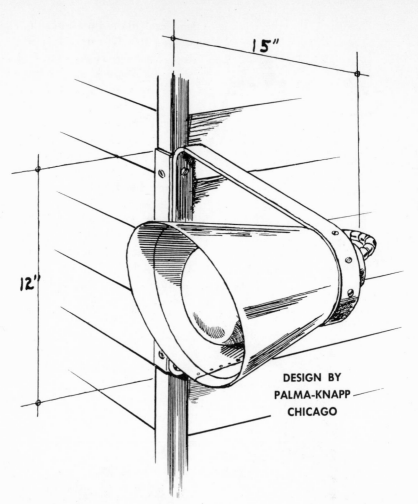

15″

12″

DESIGN BY
PALMA-KNAPP
CHICAGO

12–17

same dimensions as upper frame. Bottom, sides, and ends are cut and formed from one piece of embossed sheet 36″ x 20″ with a piece 8″ square cut out of each corner. Sides and ends are then bent up 6″ high and riveted to the upper frame. Then install ½″ plywood panel in lower frame before bolting the formed sheet box into place. Apply two coats of aluminum paint to wood before assembling.

Make each pair of legs from a 54″ length of ¼″ x 1″ bar bent to a U with 24″ for each leg, 6″ across the top. Attach with bolts through bottom of box. Braces are ⅜″ rod end-riveted to legs at "A" per *Fig. 4–20*.

TERRACE LIGHT (*Fig. 12–17*) is a modern design with simple lines. A ¹⁄₁₆″ x 1″ x 1″ angle 12″ long is riveted to a ¼″ x 1″ bar which is formed to hold the cone reflector

15″ from the house as shown. A small length of ⅛″ x ¾″ bar riveted inside the shade underneath the 1″ bar clamps the lamp socket in position. Use armored BX conductor painted with aluminum paint to prevent rust and to match the light, or use heavy-duty flexible rubber conductor.

LAMP STAND (*Fig. 12–18*) uses top frame of ¹⁄₁₆″ x 1″ x 1″ angle 6′ long, bent at all four corners as in *Fig. 4–37*, and with the two ends butted together on the back side. Top panel is ½″ plywood. Top ends of legs are bent flat and screwed against underside of top panel. Use enough screws for sturdy support. Make legs of ¼″ x 1″ bar, and rivet lower 9″ together as shown. Braces are ⅜″ rod riveted together at "A" per *Fig. 4–24*. Braces are end-riveted to legs per *Fig. 4–20*. Cover top panel with glass, or cement sheet of

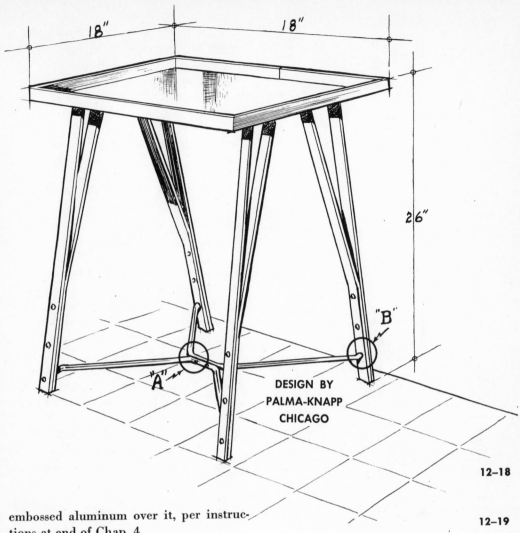

18"　　　　18"

26"

"B"

"A"

DESIGN BY
PALMA-KNAPP
CHICAGO

12–18

embossed aluminum over it, per instructions at end of Chap. 4.

12–19

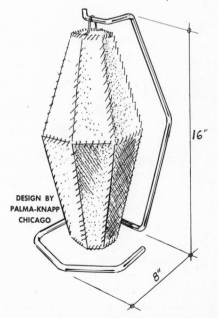

DESIGN BY
PALMA-KNAPP
CHICAGO

16"

8"

DESK LAMP (*Fig. 12–19*) uses ⅜" rod for
the frame support. Dimensions and exact
bend angles are not critical . . . . just
follow the general idea of the illustration.
For outdoor garden parties, make the
shade large enough at the bottom to fit
over a glass containing a candle. Or elec-
trify the lamp with an electric socket and
bulb. Use aluminum clothesline wire for
frame of shade and oiled parchment for
panels, which may be decorated with oil
paints or left plain.

GARDEN LUMINAIRE (*Fig. 12–20*) is easy to
make, yet presents a highly attractive
effect, since light source is below eye
level if made 3' high with 18" shade.
Others may prefer the larger size in-

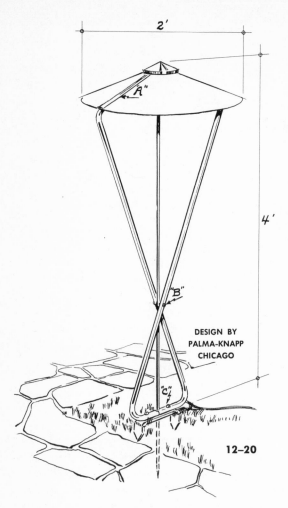

2'

"A"

4'

"B"

DESIGN BY
PALMA-KNAPP
CHICAGO

"C"

12-20

dicated. Shade is cone cut from plain or embossed sheet with lock seam at "A." See *Fig. 4–5* for details. Electric lamp socket mounts on a $3/8''$ rod center support. Side supports are $3/4''$ tube, one of which carries the electric conductor up to the lamp. Attach shade to upper section of tube with sheet-metal self-tapping screws.

Use an aluminum nail about $2\frac{1}{4}''$ long for the pin at "B." Bottom support is combination of vertical center rod and pointed ends of $1/4'' \times 1''$ bar bolted to bottom of tube as shown.

NOVELTY TABLES (*Fig. 12–21*) have many possibilities on porch or terrace, including the suggested grouping shown. These are individual triangular units, ideal for supporting potted plants or flowers, for use as seats, or as individual tables for serving tea, cocktails, or snacks. Cut three legs of $1/16'' \times 1'' \times 1''$ angle 18'' long for each table. Sharpen the 90° included angle between faces to 60° by squeezing these legs judiciously in a vise as in *Fig. 3–21*.

Next cut three 18'' lengths of the same 1'' angle for braces. Trim the horizontal

12–21

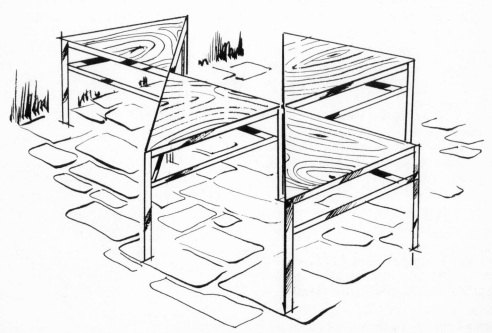

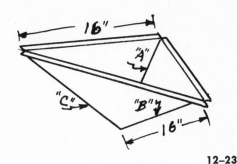

12-23

12-22

face of each piece to a 30° angle at the end so it will fit inside the leg. Assemble to legs, putting two rivets into each end of each brace, with braces down 4″ from top of legs.

Cut table top from ¾″ plywood, making equilateral triangles, 18″ on a side. Attach legs to corners of table top with long wood screws or finishing nails. Finish table top before assembling to frame.

NOVELTY PLANTER (*Fig. 12–22*) is made exactly as the table (*Fig. 12–21*) except that the table top is replaced by another set of braces, riveted to the legs. Also legs should be 16″ long, instead of 18″.

The triangular pan (*Fig. 12–23*) is made from one piece of plain aluminum sheet. It measures 16″ on a side around the top, and 16″ from each corner to bottom of pan. On a square piece of sheet 18″ x 18″, mark diagonals from opposite corners. Notch corners and bend up a 1″ flange all around. Now bend up along each diagonal to form the pan. One panel will be extra because only three of the four panels are needed for the pan. So cut off the fourth, leaving about 1″ for a

flange to overlap at "C." Thus "A" and "B" will be bends, "C" will be an overlapped joint which must now be riveted . . . . Make waterproof with mastic compound. Paint inside of planter with aluminum paint before riveting it inside the top frame.

UTILITY TABLE (*Fig. 12–24*) is ideal way to use a discarded solid door . . . . or any thick piece of wood large enough to make a table top. If nothing else is available, make table top from two or three thicknesses of ¾″ plywood, nailed or screwed together from the underside. Sand edge of table top smooth and apply a paste filler with a stain to produce a dark oak or mahogany; then varnish or finish in a flat black. Make size to suit your needs . . . . 18″ x 36″ or 42″ for cocktail tables, 18″ x 18″ for general use.

Feature of this design is the ⅜″ rod used for legs. Cut four 36″ lengths. Make 2″ radius bend 16″ from one end in each

12-24

place, leaving rods ends about 8″ apart at tips. Drill vertical holes 2″ in from each side and each end of table top to within ¼″ of upper surface of table. At a 45° angle and 6″ in from these first four holes, drill another set of four . . . . drilling vertically in both cases.

Note outside member of each leg is vertical, inside portion at an angle. Drive the short member of each leg into the outside hole; the long member into the inside hole. Be sure to bend this member 3″ from end so it will parallel short member and thus go into the vertically drilled hole. Now place the table top upside down on thin rug or a pad and force the rods into the holes, using a rubber mallet or a wood block and a hammer.

COLD FRAME (*Fig. 12–25*) is extremely light . . . . one man can easily lift and move entire unit. Top is four separate panels, each measuring 3′ x 5′ made from Do-It-Yourself Aluminum screen section fitted with plastic sheet and cross braces spaced at 1′ intervals. Sheet-metal self-tapping screws secure 18″ lengths of brace on top of the plastic sheet to the cross braces underneath. See free instruction sheets in Do-It-Yourself Aluminum racks for details on constructing plastic storm sash.

A 12′ long panel of 5-V Crimp aluminum roofing is cut to provide the enclosing structure. Its 48″ width is divided 12″ for front, 18″ for back with the remaining 18″ cut in two lengthwise to provide the ends which are then cut down to 12″ width at front, as shown in *Fig. 12–25*. Corners are joined by riveting to 12″ and 18″ lengths of $\frac{1}{16}$″ x 1″ x 1″ angle, which is also used to frame top edge of entire enclosure.

HOSE REEL (*Fig. 12–26*) uses a 6′ length of ¼″ x 1″ bar for main frame and upper handle, bent into a "U" measuring 18″ wide at top, 27″ down each side. The brace holding the unit upright is another piece of 1″ bar bent to a "U" measuring 18″ wide, 12″ down each leg. This brace is riveted to the first piece at slightly less than a 90° angle so the reel will not tip over easily.

A ⅜″ hole drilled through this connection permits passage of a 24″ length of ⅜″ rod which extends through the main frame to support two small wheels, obtained from a cycle shop. For added strength, rivet an 8″ length of 1″ bar from the bottom brace up 45° to the top or main frame.

Reel itself rotates on 20″ length of ⅜″ rod extending through a drum made by cutting two 8″ diameter circles from ¾″ plywood and nailing four 1″ x 2″ strips 16″ long between these two heads. Cover heads with plain aluminum sheet, flanged over edges. Wrap the strips with a sheet of plain aluminum 16″ wide to complete the drum. Cut two crosspieces 18″ long from ⅛″ x ¾″ bar and attach to each drumhead as shown. Make and attach a clip on one to hold the hose nozzle.

A loop of aluminum clothesline wire locks the reel when engaged with a crossbar as shown in *Fig. 12–26.* Use a 1½″ length of ¾″ tube over the reel axle between each end of the reel and the main frame to prevent reel arms from striking frame.

CHAISE LONGUE (*Fig. 12–27*) uses a frame of ¹⁄₁₆″ x 1″ x 1″ angle with corners notched and bent as in *Fig. 4–37.* Be sure to rivet splice plates inside the bend at each corner for added strength. Make frames to fit the sponge rubber cushions obtained at your nearby auto or sports goods store. Rivet ⅛″ x ¾″ bars crosswise the frame at 6″ intervals to support the cushions.

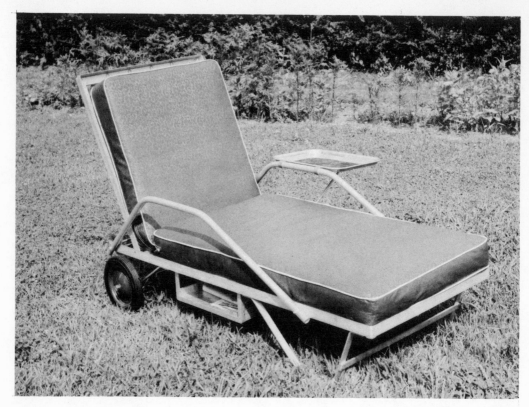

Back frame is joined to bottom frame by a single rivet or bolt at each side to allow back frame angle to be adjusted. A 6" length of ¼" x 1" bar angled down from the back frame has ⅜" slots cut into it to engage a length of ⅜" rod which extends across the extreme rear ends of the bottom frame. This allows back to be set at angle desired.

The arms of ¾" tube are bent per *Fig. 3–27* and accompanying instructions; then bolted to bottom frame. Front support for bottom frame is also ¼" x 1" bar bent and riveted to bottom frame to hold it about 8" off the ground. Be sure to add front cross brace, as pictured. Similar supports carry the back axle and the two wheels from your neighborhood cycle shop.

Handy accessories to this unit are the magazine rack underneath the bottom frame . . . . made from ⅛" x ¾" angle and sheet. The left arm has clips and an angle support of ⅜" rod bent and riveted to a tray obtained from the corner dime store.

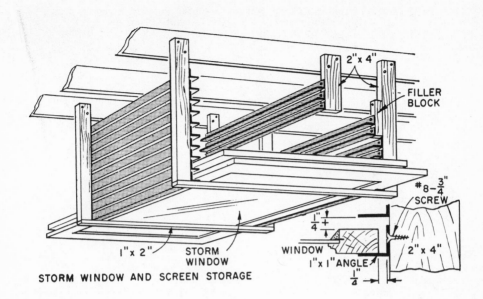

STORM WINDOW AND SCREEN STORAGE

Chapter 13 . . .

PROJECTS FOR HOME IMPROVEMENT

SCREEN-STORAGE RACK (*Fig. 13–1*) stores screens or storm windows overhead in garage or basement. Vertical supports are 2 x 4's nailed to ceiling joists in garage or underside of floor joists in basement. Measure screens or windows, and make the distance between supports equal to their width plus ¼″ for side clearance. Nail 1 x 2's across bottom ends of vertical supports to keep them from spreading.

The slides are 1/16″ x 1″ x 1″ aluminum angle, attached to the supports by drilling 5/32″ holes and countersinking so #8 x ¾″ aluminum screws will seat flush. Space the slides ¼″ apart (1¼″ between horizontal faces).

To hold narrow screens or windows, add more vertical supports inside original verticals as shown in *Fig. 13–1*.

PARTITION (*Fig. 13–2*) makes an attractive unit to divide off various areas in the basement, rumpus room, office, or workshop. The panels are ordinary corrugated aluminum such as is used for roofing or siding. Or they may be panels with small holes perforated in them . . . . known as acoustical panels.

In either case, paint them with a flat paint in a soft color to match your decorative scheme, or retain the original bright aluminum finish and avoid finger marking by applying a coat of wax.

Vertical supports are 1″ or 1¼″ tube which can be mounted directly into the floor and ceiling or fitted into 2″ x 4″ pieces which in turn mount to floor and ceiling. Join tubes end to end where necessary per *Fig. 4–63*.

Sheet-metal self-tapping screws are excellent for securing the panels to the tube.

To obtain sound deadening, use two of the perforated panels with a layer of glass wool or other acoustical material sandwiched in between them. Do not apply

paint to such an assembly . . . . paint the panels before assembling.

CARD TABLE RENOVATED: To hide the battered top of your old card table, cover it with leather-grained embossed aluminum sheet. Then hot dishes or wet glasses can be set directly on the top without dam-

aging it. Stains and spilled food wipe up in a jiffy.

Place embossed aluminum sheet face down on floor, and lay table, top down, over it as shown in *Fig. 13–3*. Allow sufficient material around each side to fold over the frame as shown in the cross section at the top. Notch corners and around

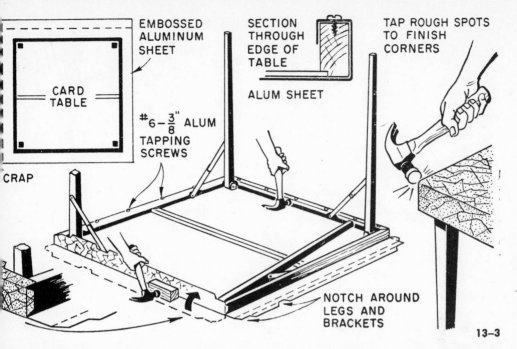

EMBOSSED ALUMINUM SHEET

CARD TABLE

CRAP

#6 – 3/8" ALUM TAPPING SCREWS

SECTION THROUGH EDGE OF TABLE

ALUM SHEET

TAP ROUGH SPOTS TO FINISH CORNERS

NOTCH AROUND LEGS AND BRACKETS

13–3

egs and brackets. Bend up first flange along sides, using a hammer and wood block as shown. Tap corners gently to smooth edges. Secure to frame with screws. Bend aluminum over and down inside frame to avoid catching on clothes.

Finish by coating top and sides with clear lacquer or paste wax, polished well.

HI-FI RADIO-PHONOGRAPH (*Fig. 13–4*) is simple to construct with 3/4" plywood lacquered in black and with satin-finished

13–4

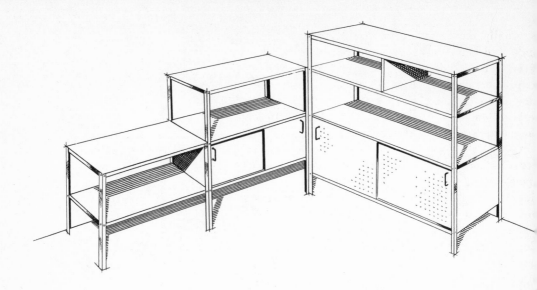

frame of $\frac{1}{16}''$ x 1" x 1" angle. See *Fig. 4–37* for corner bends. Front instrument panel is Masonite, painted white. Ornamental aluminum strips above radio dial and below amplifier controls at left are plain aluminum sheets, cemented to Masonite, scratch-marked into squares, and swirled by rubbing with circular strokes in each square, per *Fig. 5–3*.

Cabinet is dimensioned according to your equipment. Leave the bottom of speaker cabinet open to avoid cabinet resonance. It is important to line the speaker cabinet with 1" or 2" layer of glass wool or other acoustic material.

MODULAR CABINETS (*Fig. 13–5*) offer endless design combinations. Height and length can be varied. Sections can be fitted with or without doors . . . . either sliding (see *Fig. 4–82*) or hinge type. But to get the benefit of modular design and use material efficiently, make them all 12" deep, front to back, and make them either 3' or 4' long. If made as individual units, they can easily be rearranged for various room groupings. Left unit is 3' high; right, 4' high.

Make legs of either $\frac{1}{8}''$ x $\frac{3}{4}''$ x $\frac{3}{4}''$ or $\frac{1}{16}''$ x 1" x 1" angle, using the same size for all your units. Frame top shelf with the same angle if you wish. All shelves and panels are $\frac{3}{4}''$ plywood. Include in

each cabinet at least one full box section. Back panel will then provide lateral rigidity; end panels, the front-to-back rigidity needed for a steady structure. This eliminates the need for braces.

Shelf heights should match for all your units, although box sections may differ. Here the right unit has an 18" high box (outside) 4" from floor, 14" to top of next shelf, 12" more to top of cabinet. The left cabinet has a 16" high box 6' from floor. Turn leg ends under to avoid digging into floor, per *Fig. 4–49*.

KICK PLATES help protect lower parts of outside doors, and especially the inside of screen doors where the youngsters kick them open. Cover these areas with an attractive sheet of embossed aluminum, nailed or screwed in place.

STAIR RAILS are an important safety item. Equip every stairway in your house with rails of $1\frac{1}{4}''$ aluminum tube, attached to the wall per *Fig. 4–79*. Close open ends with snap-in plugs available at all Do-It-Yourself Aluminum outlets, or fit wood dowels.

HANDLES for everything from garbage cans to toolboxes, as well as door handles, shelf braces, etc., are easy to make to order. Select a piece of aluminum tube; $\frac{3}{4}''$ size s usually most convenient. Flatten both ends, and bend to form handle. Screw or rivet to object desired. Or another type handle is made by flattening ¾" tube enough so that ⅛" x ¾" bar can be inserted. Bend ends of bar down to form attachment, and screw or rivet to object.

SCREENS for all windows in your house are easy to make with special screen sections found in all Do-It-Yourself Aluminum racks. Corners are made simply by pushing clips into hollow frame members. Complete instructions are available there free and are not duplicated here because of space limitations. Investigate this easy-to-make framing system. There is no tacking of screen wire, as wedges lock screen into frames (see *Fig. 13–6*).

SCREEN PORCH OR BREEZEWAY: Any porch can easily be screened in completely with Do-It-Yourself screen sections. Divide porch or breezeway sides into panels 24" or 36" wide. Install 2" x 4" frames edgewise, per *Fig. 13–6*, and rabbet outer corners ⁷⁄₁₆" deep, ½" wide, to take the screen frames. Turn buttons made from 2" lengths of ⅛" x ¾" bar lock the screen panels into the wood frames. For full-

13–6

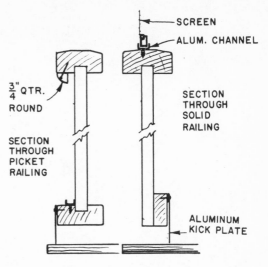

13–7

height screens, install a horizontal rail all around the porch at 30" height. Then use screens below and another set above rail.

For stub-wall porches with picket railings, set ¾" quarter-round under top rail and channel on top bottom rail as at left (*Fig. 13–7*) for holding screen panels. Screw on strips of embossed sheet to lower rail to close opening to floor. Install an aluminum channel along the top of the upper rail to receive screen panels. Use vertical meeting rails of 2" x 4" every 36" (or less as needed to make equal panel sizes).

STORM WINDOWS: Do-It-Yourself Aluminum racks offer two ways of making storm windows and storm-door closures . . . . with glass or with sheets of clear plastic. The racks also contain detailed free instruction sheets for both materials, so there is no need to repeat directions here. One frame member is joined at corners with bolts; the other, with clips pushed into the hollow member. Both types are simple and easy to make.

STORM DOORS: Any screen door is easily converted into a weatherproof storm door by installing panels carrying a sheet of clear plastic in an aluminum frame . . . . made exactly the same way as storm windows described fully in instruction

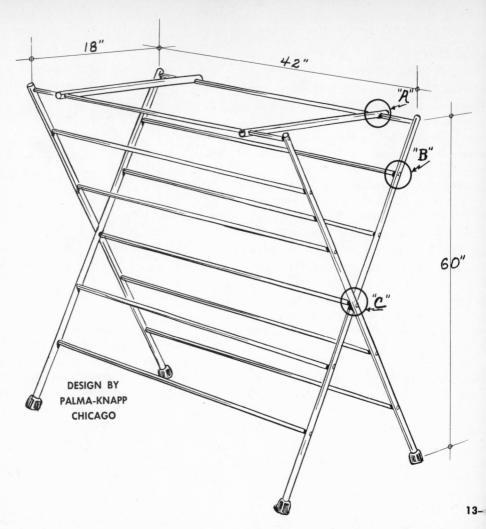

18"

42"

"A"

"B"

60"

"C"

DESIGN BY
PALMA-KNAPP
CHICAGO

13-

sheets available free at the Do-It-Yourself Aluminum racks.

PUSH RODS to save screen doors are easily made of ¾″ or 1″ tube, bent down and flattened at each end for screwing to door frame.

SCREEN-DOOR BRACE: To keep screen doors from sagging and sticking, cut a length of ⅛″ x ¾″ bar and attach it diagonally from the lower outside corner of screen door up at a 45° angle to the opposite side of screen door. Insert three round-head wood screws in each end to anchor securely. Wedge up outer edge of door when installing the brace on a door already sagging and sticking.

FOLDING CLOTHES RACK (*Fig. 13–8*) uses for the legs four 65″ long pieces of ¾″

tube and two 20″ lengths for the top crosspieces. The other 11 pieces are ⅜″ rod, six cut 43½″ long and five cut 42″ long. Prepare these rods for assembly by reducing a ¼″ section at both ends of all 11 rods to ³⁄₁₆″ diameter, per *Fig. 4–16*. Prepare legs to receive them by drilling a ³⁄₁₆″ hole 1″ from the top end clear through leg. Then follow by enlarging the hole on the inside of the leg to ⅜″ diameter with a drill of that size. Now insert end of one rod, and upset outer end to make a solid riveted connection per *Fig. 4–21*. Notice that the five short rods go on "inside" legs, the six long ones on the "outside" legs. Now measure down 10″, and make connection at "B" in the same manner. All other rods are tied into the legs in the same manner except the center one at "C."

Here a ⅜″ hole is drilled clear through

116

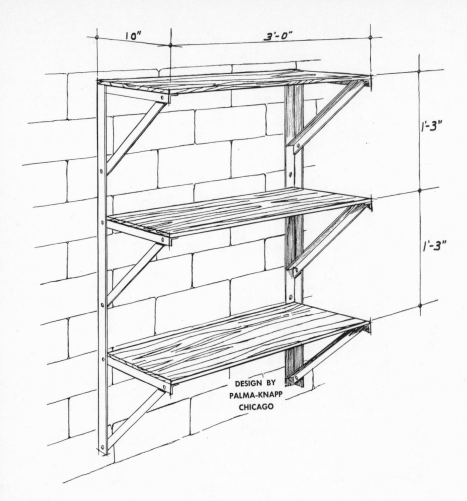

10" 3'-0"

1'-3"

1'-3"

DESIGN BY
PALMA-KNAPP
CHICAGO

13–9

the inside leg as well, so the rod is riveted to the outside leg only. This allows the rack to be folded without twisting any of the connections. Two top crossbars ($\frac{3}{4}''$ tube) have $\frac{3}{8}''$ holes drilled 1" in from one end. Be sure to slide these tubes onto top bar before end-riveting that bar into the two legs. At the other end of these crossbars, saw a notch in the bottom to latch into the top rod at "A." Add rubber crutch tips to the feet to complete the unit.

STORAGE SHELVES: *Figure 13–9* shows a method of attaching a series of shelves to basement wall, garage, back porch, or any other spot where some wall space may be available. Use $\frac{1}{8}''$ x $\frac{3}{4}''$ x $\frac{3}{4}''$ angle for the supporting framework. If the wall is masonry, use a Stellite drill in a portable electric drill or make holes by hand with

star chisel and hammer. Insert expanding lead sleeves or other masonry attachment device available at your local hardware store.

STEPLADDER (*Fig. 13–10*) offers amazing lightness yet ample strength when made of $\frac{1}{8}''$ x $\frac{3}{4}''$ x $\frac{3}{4}''$ angle, $\frac{3}{4}''$ tube, and $\frac{1}{8}''$ x $\frac{3}{4}''$ bar as marked on the drawing. Individual steps are 12" long, 5" deep, supported underneath the front edge by an angle riveted to side frame members. Start this project by cutting the top step 10" x 15" from $\frac{3}{4}''$ plywood. Cut an 18" length of $\frac{1}{4}''$ x 1" bar, turn down $1\frac{1}{2}''$ at each end, and screw to underside of top. Attach the back legs, 6' lengths of $\frac{3}{4}''$ tube, to this bracket with bolts, using two nuts locked against each other to permit movement of leg against bracket.

Assemble each side frame from two 6'

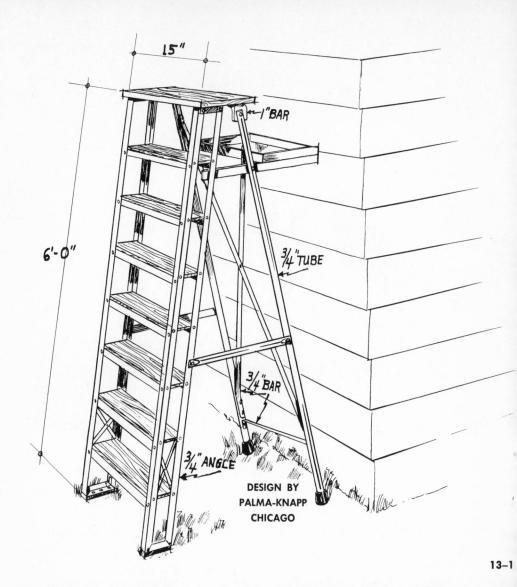

15"

1" BAR

6'-0"

3/4" TUBE

3/4" BAR

3/4" ANGLE

DESIGN BY
PALMA-KNAPP
CHICAGO

13-1

lengths of ¾″ angle with 5″ long stretch-ers at extreme top and bottom, riveted in place. Now rivet the 15″ lengths of ¾″ angle between the two side frames, 9″ apart, to support the steps. At this point, screw the upper stretcher of each side frame to the underside of the top panel. Attach the braces between the two back legs, and install the side braces between front and back legs as directed below. (Note that these are notched over bolts on the back legs so they can be unhooked for folding up the ladder.)

Now with frame assembled, stand it up with back legs 3′ from front legs on the floor. Cut side braces (¾″ tube) to the correct length at this point, flatten ends,

bolt to front frame, and notch. Adjus side frames so top panel lies horizontally and attach bottom step, screwing through front stretcher into underside of ste along front, setting a long screw into bac of step through back member of sid frame with step positioned horizontally Install a second step in the same manner Add ⅛″ x ¾″ bar cross braces to sid frame now, and mount in the other steps All steps are ½″ plywood. Be sure to coa with sealer before assembling them int frame.

Put rubber crutch tips on back legs screw rubber-faced block underneat front legs.

AWNINGS (*Fig. 13–11*) are suitable for porch or window. This is a simplified design that employs panels of aluminum which have been formed to look like ordinary wood clapboard siding. These panels are a standard product available at most building supply outlets. It is a simple matter to make an attractive awning using them. Corrugated or 5-V Crimp panels are also suitable.

Panels 2′ wide are large enough for most people, although some prefer 3′ wide . . . . the size shown in *Fig. 13–11*. Cut to length required by porch or window. Frame ends and bottom edge with ⅛″ x ¾″ x ¾″ angle underneath and flush with edge of panel, using self-tapping sheet-metal screws.

For permanent installation, bend up a ?″ flange along top edge so it lies flat against house. Secure it to house by putting Do-It-Yourself Aluminum trim strip on this flange and screwing through it into the wood with ordinary aluminum round-head screws.

After attaching top edge of awning to house, pull awning out to a 45° angle and measure horizontally to determine length required for brace, starting from a point about 6″ from bottom edge of awning. Cut a ⅛″ x ¾″ x ¾″ angle to this length plus 1″. Cut and bend one end as in *Fig. 4–47*. Screw this end to house a distance down from top of awning equal to length of brace. Now extend brace horizontally to awning frame and rivet.

BRACKET FOR HOUSE NUMBERS (*Fig. 13–12*) uses ⅛″ x ¾″ bar. Start by cutting top slanting member 21″ long and curling ends on ¾″ radius per *Fig. 3–14*. Next cut a piece 24″ long and make a 90° bend in it 14″ from one end. This is bottom member of bracket. Now rivet lower end of first member to long end of second member in approximate position shown in *Fig. 13–12*.

Cut another 24″ piece of the ¾″ bar and form the "S" scroll per *Fig. 3–18*, using about a 1″ radius for small curve,

119

3″ radius for large curve. After forming to shape desired, fit into bracket frame, saw off any extra metal, and rivet to top slanting member.

Cut ¾″ plywood panel 5″ x 12″, paint black and mount house numbers on it. Obtain these at your hardware or dime store, or cut from embossed sheet using your old house numbers as a pattern. Attach letters to panel with small aluminum tacks or brads. Secure wood panel to bracket with round-head wood screws where scroll contacts lower bracket member. If vertical section is too long, cut off excess. Then attach to house with round-head wood screws as indicated.

Laundry Chute (*Fig. 13–13*) will not ru▮ clothes and prevents them from milde▮ ing. Use perforated sheet for the panel the union jack design being shown her Make frame from ⅟₁₆″ x 1″ x 1″ angle joining corners as shown in *Fig. 4–43*, an using the framing system of *Fig. 4–42.*

Door is ¼″ plywood, hinged at the bo▮ tom for easy removal of clothes. Locat▮ chute directly below a circular hole ▮ floor cut to take gunny sack or flour sac▮ which has bottom cut out and is tacke▮ just inside floor opening. A hook on wa▮ supports top of sack. Or locate sack in cupboard to keep it from view. Or co▮ struct a plywood chute to feed containe▮

13–13

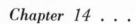

Chapter 14 . . .

PROJECTS FOR THE CHILDREN

CHILD'S TABLE AND CHAIR SET (*Fig. 14–1*) will greatly enhance any child's room and provide an excellent work and play center. For the table, cut out and screw or nail together two pieces of ¾" plywood 24" x 30". Pine Nov-A-Ply makes a beautiful surface pattern and is recommended for the top piece. In each corner, drill 1" diameter holes for the legs 2" in from each edge of the table top, drilling vertically into underside of table to a depth of 1¼".

Inlay edge of table with 1⁄16" x 1" x 1" angle per *Fig. 4–50*. Apply in two pieces, each extending full length of one side and half the width of the table at each end (54¼"). File one end of each piece smooth and square. Make corner bends

as directed in *Fig. 4–37*, starting the first 12⅛" in from the end just prepared. Fit length between bends per instructions in Chap. 4. Proceed to attach first piece of angle to table.

Then cut and fit other piece. After bending, trim ends to make exact fit with first piece of inlay already in place.

Cut four 21" legs for the table from 1" tube. Smooth off one end of each leg, and insert per instructions with *Fig. 4–57*. Place on flat surface, and trim longest leg so that table sets evenly. Close open ends of legs with snap-in end fittings.

For the chair, cut and nail or screw together two pieces of ¾" plywood 12" x 14". Place this seat upside down, and mark hole centers 1¼" in from each edge.

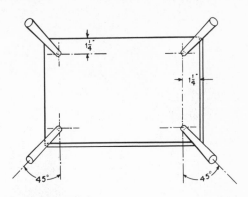

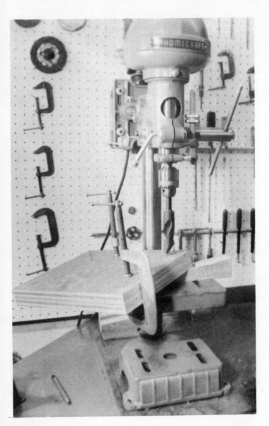

14–2

Notice that chair legs are at an angle, not vertical, for best footing and appearance (10° is used here). The back legs extend straight backward. The front legs do not extend straight forward or straight out sidewise but out 45° cornerwise, as shown in *Fig. 14–3*.

Since back legs extend through seat to form a frame for seat back, drill these holes clear through the seat, using the 10° wedge when clamping to bed of drill press. To get a little clearance for easy insertion of the tube, wobble the rotating drill in the hole slightly or run it through several times to enlarge the hole slightly.

For front legs, clamp seat on bed of drill press as shown in *Fig. 14–2*, using the 10° wedge to get the angle desired. Set drill stop for a depth of 1⅜″.

Cut front legs 12½″ long from 1″ tube. Insert the same way as table legs. Lock in position with finishing nails 2½″ long driven in from edge of seat. Drill clearance holes slightly smaller than nail

shank and just 1½″ deep to assure penetrating the tube wall. Drive the nail which will pierce far wall of tube and pass on into wood, securely locking tube. Put four nails into each leg, one near the center of each piece of plywood in the seat, from each edge.

Cut back legs 26½″ long from 1″ tube. At a point 14″ from one end, make a 22½° bend on a 9″ radius, per instructions in *Fig. 3–27*. Insert these legs through seat, putting the 14″ end through from the top side. Lubricate with wax or old candle. If hole has not sufficient clearance to permit insertion, wobble drill in hole as suggested above. Position legs so they extend through seat the same distance as front legs. Turn tubes in seat so that bent portion extends straight backward. Then lock each back leg to seat with four nails as previously described.

Upholster the seat with a layer of cotton batting, covered with plastic sheet material, folded and tacked under the seat at front, back, and both sides. Holes are cut to fit the back seat frame.

Use any heavy fabric material for the seat back. First sew a narrow hem at top and bottom (about 10″ in height). Then sew a wide hem on each end, big enough to slip over the frame formed by the extension of the back legs. Close top end of this hem so tube end will not come through. Fit so seat back is tight when slipped over the tube.

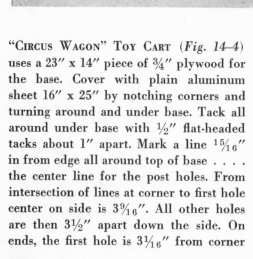

"Circus Wagon" Toy Cart (*Fig. 14–4*) uses a 23″ x 14″ piece of ¾″ plywood for the base. Cover with plain aluminum sheet 16″ x 25″ by notching corners and turning around and under base. Tack all around under base with ½″ flat-headed tacks about 1″ apart. Mark a line $^{15}/_{16}$″ in from edge all around top of base . . . . the center line for the post holes. From intersection of lines at corner to first hole center on side is $3^9/_{16}$″. All other holes are then 3½″ apart down the side. On ends, the first hole is $3^1/_{16}$″ from corner

intersection; the others, 3″ apart. After marking hole centers, drill ¾″ holes through aluminum and ½″ into plywood with an ordinary brace and bit, per *Fig. 2–17*.

Top rail is $^1/_{16}$″ x 1″ x 1″ angle 70″ long. Drill a $^3/_{32}$″ hole for bending corners at 22″ from one end, another at 35″, a third at 57″. Notch and bend per *Fig. 4–37*. Mark tube locations the same as base. Cut 20 pieces of ¾″ tube exactly $10^5/_8$″ long. Insert tubes in base, drill ⅛″ holes from edge of base toward the center

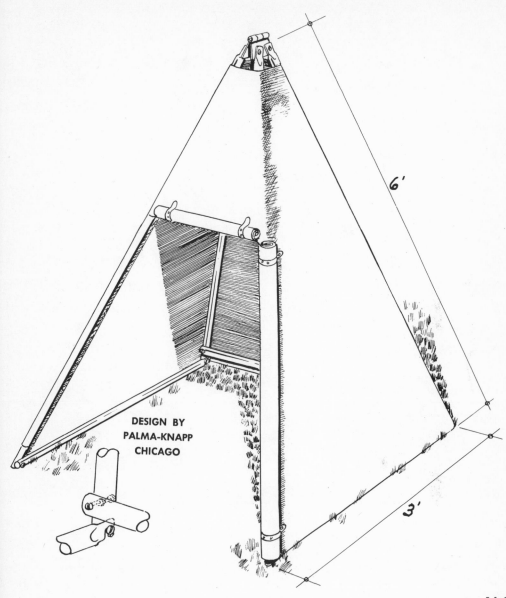

6'

3'

DESIGN BY
PALMA-KNAPP
CHICAGO

14–5

of each tube, and drive a #8 x ¾″ self-tapping screw. Drill ⅛″ holes through top rail into top of tubes, and insert #6 x ½″ self-tapping screws.

For top curls, bend (per *Fig. 3–18*) four 18″ lengths of ⅛″ x ¾″ bar to a ½″ radius on one end, 1⅜″ radius on other; attach to top rail with bolts. Tongue is a 15″ length of ¾″ tube set between a pair of angles cut from ¾″ bar, 1¾″ on a side. Put four 2″ furniture casters on underside of base. Make four 4″ diameter wheels of ¾″ plywood. Attach wheel rims

of ¾″ strips of plain sheet. Paint star and scallops on wheels. Paint and cut out clown design (or any other design desired) on sides from plain sheet. Attach to tubes with self-tapping screws.

PLAY TENT (*Fig. 14–5*) will give the youngsters no end of fun. Dimensions suggested, of course, may be enlarged easily if desired to make room for beds. Use 1¼″ tube for the four 6′ main members, ¾″ tube for the three 36″ spacers at ground level. Bolt one end of each

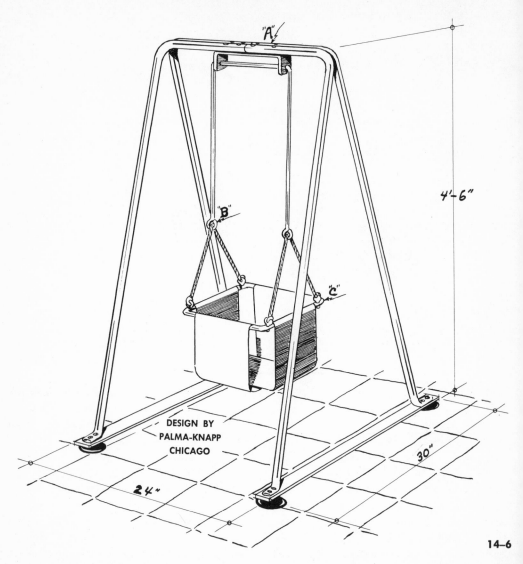

"A"

4'-6"

"B"

"C"

DESIGN BY
PALMA-KNAPP
CHICAGO

24"

30"

14-6

spacer directly to the bottom of a main frame member, but use an extra nut on the bolt between the two tubes so that some play can be left in the joint to permit folding up the connection without loosening the bolt. See the inset of *Fig. 14–5*.

At the other end of each spacer, flatten out a 2″ section and saw a notch in it to latch over a bolt extended out from the 1¼″ tube to which it is connected as shown by *Fig. 14–5*. This then allows the entire frame to be folded up without removing or loosening any bolts.

The top end of each of the four main frame members is flattened by squeezing in a vise, then riveted to a 3½″ or 4″

hinge. Now get Mother to help in cutting and fitting a heavy canvas covering to the frame. Sew straps to the bottom edge of covering and to the door opening to tie around frame members.

CHILD'S SWING (*Fig. 14–6*) is a handy place for the baby, as it can be moved about the house easily to be in sight of Mother. Baby will enjoy it, too. Main A-frames are four 6′ lengths of ¾″ tube, flattened at the bottom end for riveting to a 32″ length of ¼″ x 1″ bar forming the bottom stretcher on each side. Attach rubber suction cups as shown to keep swing from "walking" when in use. Bending off a 12″ piece at the top end of

126

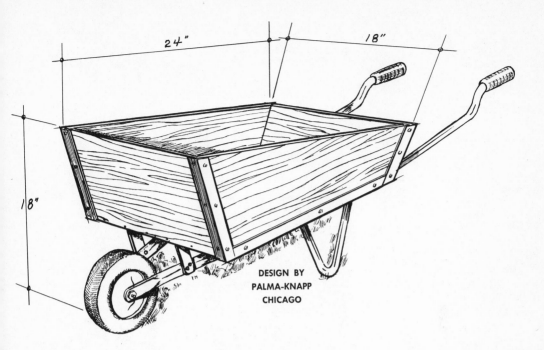

24″ 18″

18″

DESIGN BY
PALMA-KNAPP
CHICAGO

each leg gives a height of about 54″. See *Fig. 3–27* and accompanying instructions for tube bending.

Join legs by bolting to the U-shaped piece of ¼″ x 1″ bar stock at "A" which is 12″ across top, 2″ down each side. It has ⅜″ holes for the swing rod which is turned up at "B" for the short lengths of cord or chain supporting the seat. Frame for seat is ⅜″ rod formed to a 12″ square, ends halved and riveted per *Fig. 4–22*. Cover with canvas as shown. Attach large screw eyes to frame by drilling, screwing through, and upsetting on opposite side to lock securely.

CHILD'S WHEELBARROW (*Fig. 14–7*) will supply the youngster with many an opportunity to help Dad outdoors. Suggested dimensions may be reduced to 14″ high, 18″ long, 14″ wide if desired. Bottom of box section is ¾″ plywood; sides and ends are ¼″ plywood. Corner angles are 1/16″ x 1″ x 1″. The ¾″ tube for the handles is flattened at the front end for the wheel connection. A U-shaped bracket of ¼″ x 1″ bar bolted to the two tubes just back of the wheel supports front end

of box. Tubes then extend on back to the V-bend forming the back legs, back up to the box and then to the handles. Bolt tube to bottom of box at top of V-bend. Attach rubber bicycle grips to form handles as shown. See *Fig. 3–27* and accompanying instructions for tube bending.

JOLLY HORSE (*Fig. 14–8*) uses 30″ length of ¾″ tube for main member. Flatten rear end and bolt to it a U-shaped piece of ⅛″ x ¾″ bar formed to go around the cylinder. This is made from two 6″ diameter circles of ¾″ plywood with ten 8″ lengths of ⅜″ rod fitted into holes on a circle ¾″ inside edge of wood end pieces. Drill these ⅜″ holes just ½″ deep. Drive all ten rods into one end piece, then insert two or three small sleigh bells and drive other end piece onto the rods. Attach U-bar to cylinder with round-head wood screws into center of wood ends. Avoid setting screws so tightly that cylinder cannot turn easily.

Cut out horse head from ¾″ plywood, carefully rounding all edges, smoothing entire surface, and painting as shown. Flatten upper end of tube member and

screw to underside of horse head. A small bright red strap will finish it off.

TINKLE WHEELBARROW (*Fig. 14–9*) uses same cylinder with bells in it as described above (*Fig. 14–8*). Wheelbarrow itself uses two 30″ lengths of ⅛″ x ¾″ x ¾″ angle for main members which extend from cylinder, under body of barrow and back to form the two handles. The legs

are 20″ lengths of ⅛″ x ¾″ bar formed to a V of 8″ on a side with bottom 1″ wide and 1½″ flanged on each end for riveting to the main members.

Make pan from one piece of plain sheet, following box design explained in *Fig. 3–7*. Here, of course, box is not square. End toward handles is only 1″ high, 14″ wide. Opposite end is 3″ high, 11″ wide at bottom, 12″ wide at top. Sides slant to

join ends. Turn over a ½″ flange on all top edges and carefully smooth all corners and sheet edges. Front corners are locked with ½″ flange on side members overlapping front end and riveted per *Fig. 4–7.*

14–10

TRICYCLE LIFT (*Fig. 14–10*) will fascinate many a youngster with its possibilities. Here it is used for pulling a wagon. It will also lift and carry boxes, baskets, and other packages. Main member is 3′ length of 1¼″ tube, flattened at bottom end and bolted to rear foot stand or around rear axle. Side braces are 32″ lengths of ¾″ tube, flattened at top for bolting to main member. Bottom ends are also flattened and drilled to take axle. Wheels are re-moved, these members placed over axle and wheels replaced.

Top brace is 30″ length of ¾″ tube, flattened at top for bolting to main member and flattened at bottom for bolting to seat post. Attach a small galvanized pulley to upper end of main frame with a "U" member made from ⅛″ x ¾″ bar stock as shown. Thread a piece of clothesline through it and your young teamster is ready for action.

Chapter 15 . . .

COST ESTIMATING

OFTEN when working out a design or considering a project, you may wish to know the cost of the material required for it. The following table presents typical costs of Do-It-Yourself Aluminum on a per-square-foot basis for sheet items and a per-linear-foot basis for tube, rod, bar, and similar items. While these may vary somewhat with your particular locality and with general price trends, they will serve to provide rough cost estimates.

Plain sheet . . . . 27¢ per square foot
Embossed sheet . . . . 30¢ per square foot
Perforated sheet . . . 33¢ per square foot
⅛″ x ¾″ bar . . . . . . 27¢ per linear foot
¼″ x 1″ bar . . . . . . 33¢ per linear foot
1″ x 1″ x ⅟₁₆″ angle . 32¢ per linear foot
¾″ x ¾″ x ⅛″ angle 28¢ per linear foot
¾″ diameter tube . . . 25¢ per linear foot
1″ diameter tube . . . 27¢ per linear foot
1¼″ diameter tube . 33¢ per linear foot
⅜″ diameter round
    rod . . . . 20¢ per linear foot
Screen section with
    spline . . . . 19¢ per linear foot
Screen cross brace . . . 13¢ per linear foot
Storm sash section . . 21¢ per linear foot

Hardware kits:
  Screws, hangers,
    and hooks for
    screen for a
    window . . . . 39¢ per kit
  Screws, bolts,
    brackets, and
    hangers for
    single storm sash
    for a window . . . 69¢ per kit

SPECIAL SOURCES
Mirror-finished
  aluminum sheet . . Metal Goods Corp.
                      640 Rosedale Ave.
                      St. Louis, Mo.

INDEX